NARRATIVES
OF THE
Nativity

Blessings in Christ

D. Mueller

NARRATIVES
OF THE
Nativity
as told by those who experienced them

a first hand account
written by Del Mueller

TATE PUBLISHING & *Enterprises*

Published by Tate Publishing & Enterprises, LLC
127 E. Trade Center Terrace | Mustang, Oklahoma 73064 USA
1.888.361.9473 | www.tatepublishing.com

Tate Publishing is committed to excellence in the publishing industry. The company reflects the philosophy established by the founders, based on Psalm 68:11,
"The Lord gave the word and great was the company of those who published it."

Book design copyright © 2009 by Tate Publishing, LLC. All rights reserved.
Cover and Interior design by Elizabeth A. Mason
Illustration by Greg White

Published in the United States of America

ISBN: 978-1-60696-428-6
1. Religion: Biblical Studies: Bible Study Guides
2. Fiction: Historical
09.01.23

To my wife,
Dorleen;
my children,
Christine, Paul, Lois, Susan;
their spouses;
and my grandchildren,
Emily, Brandon, Rachel, Michael,
Luke, Mitchell, Megan,
& Jacob

INTRODUCTION

The story you are about to read may be considered a historical novel. Its intent is to assist the reader to develop a more complete understanding of the Nativity through use of a *quasi-historical* approach. I have written about the events of the Nativity as I imagine the various characters *who lived* the biblical story may have described them. Therefore, this is a theoretical *firsthand* account of the events related to Christ's birth, told by the persons who witnessed them.

The two authorities on which this story is based are St. Matthew and St. Luke, writers of the first and third gospels. Since Matthew was one of Jesus' disciples, he had face-to-face contact with the Lord. However, since Luke never met Jesus during the thirty-plus years Christ was on earth, he needed to learn the details of Jesus' life from those who had witnessed it.

Luke's Gospel is a letter written to an acquaintance of high rank by the name of Theophilus. It was Luke's spoken intent to write a report of the things that took place related to Jesus Christ, whom Luke regarded as the Messiah—Christ—Anointed One, and Joshua—Jesus—Savior.

Luke was aware that many people had written of the things that had taken place among them as related to Jesus. He posits, "They wrote what we have been told by those who saw these things from the beginning and who proclaimed the message" (Luke 1:2). It appears that following this model Luke gathered his data through interview. He very probably spent time with Jesus' mother, Mary; with Peter and John; possibly with Matthew; Mary Magdalene; Joanna; Mary Salome; Lazarus, Mary, and Martha; Mark's mother, Mary; and certainly with Mark himself since they and Paul were together in Rome.

In Luke's introductory remarks, he states, "Your Excellency, because I have carefully studied all these matters from their beginning, I thought it would be good to write an orderly account for you. I do this so that you will know the full truth about everything which you have been taught" (Luke 1:3).

Building from the approach used by Luke, I have tried to tell the biblical story accurately, attempting to assure that nothing in the narrative conflicted directly with what is recorded in the Holy Scriptures. However, to make the story flow, it became necessary to provide anecdotal information where no detail was offered in Holy Scripture. Where this happened, I have invented actions and dialogue that, to me, seemed a reasonable possibility.

Examples of such actions and dialogue are: events associated with Zechariah burning incense in the temple; Mary visiting Elizabeth; Mary returning to Nazareth pregnant; wise men visiting the holy family; and the flight to Egypt, to name a few.

I gave the names Joachim and Anne to Mary's parents since these have been the traditional names assigned to them over time. I detailed the interior of Herod's temple as best as I could determine based on literature I was able to research. Following tradition, I placed Mary's birth in Jerusalem. While there is no reference to Bar Mitzvah in Scripture, I assumed a similar rite of passage was practiced in Jesus' day. So that spoken content taken directly from Scripture might be stated in contemporary format. The Good News Bible was used when quoting or paraphrasing.

It may be assumed that some anecdotal narrative is poorly chosen and some imagined actions are not sufficiently supported by known facts. My purpose for this book is to help the reader gain a comprehensive overview of the activities related to the Nativity of our Lord, providing a story line that flows from event to event. I ask the reader to pardon any errors and thus enjoy my version of the episodes related to the birth of our Savior.

THEN ZECHARIAH SAID

I am absolutely convinced that angels are real! I know this because of what happened to me.

I can't say that I didn't believe before, but believing and being absolutely convinced were for me a contrast in conviction. Before that fateful day, I believed because of what I had been told by my parents and my rabbi, and as an adult, by the Pharisees who taught in the House of Hillel. Now

I believe because I was there; I was physically in the presence of the angel Gabriel!

But I am getting ahead of myself.

My ancestry can be traced back to Levi and through Aaron, the brother of Moses. I am a Jewish priest. My office falls under the order of Abijah, the eighth of the twenty-four orders into which priests are divided. I am married to a good woman, Elizabeth, who also is a member of a priestly family.

My tenure as priest has been long. Both of us are old, certainly past the age of childbearing. We are considered good and godly people who do their best to obey the laws and commands of our beloved Jehovah.

Twice each year I have the privilege of traveling to Jerusalem; it's only a day's journey from our town, Ein Karem. While in Jerusalem I spend one week serving as priest in the holy temple. During that week I live in one of the chambers set apart for priests, located just adjacent to the temple proper.

It is truly a privilege and an honor to serve as priest in the holy temple. Each day worshippers bring gifts as offerings to Yahweh. Some offerings are presented to God in order to confess guilt and to ask for forgiveness. Other offerings are presented as a way of praising God, giving him thanks, and showing a personal commitment to him. The gifts set before us may be animals, grains, vegetables, incense, and of course, money.

Priests consider the most cherished temple service to be the Offering of Incense. At the beginning of the week, one priest is chosen by lot to perform this honor, and a priest can be chosen only once in his lifetime. I had the good fortune to be selected.

This is why I know that angels are real:

That *life-changing* day was a Sabbath, my last service as priest of the incense. I entered, as usual, through the Coporius Gate into the temple, walked proudly through the Court of the Gentiles and up the thirteen steps leading to the Court of the Women. There I entered the vestment antechamber with its baths for my ritual purification washing. My Levite assistants were already there, three preparing the spices while the taper bearer trimmed his candlewick. We dressed. I put on my priestly garments, first the pants, then the tunic, next the belt, and finally the turban.

As twilight approached, my assistants and I performed the ritual washing of our hands, bowed in prayer as preparation, poured a mixture of frankincense and oil onto the charcoal-covered bottom of the golden sensor, and lit the sweet mix. I then picked up the golden chain holding the censer, and gently swinging the incense from side to side, left the antechamber, and with my four Levites, processed past the thirteen horn-shaped treasury receptacles, where worshippers deposited temple money.

After ascending the fifteen-step rounded stairway, we entered the Nicanor Gate that led to the Court of Israel. We continued past the balustrade separation and entered the Court of the Priests. After striding past the horned sacrificial altar with its ramp, and the bronze laver next to the slaughter area, we approached the holy place.

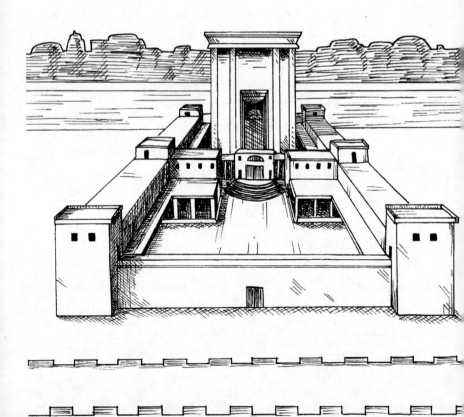

As we reached the last of twelve steps and entered the portico to the holy place, I could see the golden table of showbread, the golden menorah, and the golden altar of incense set directly before the great curtain that prevented all but the high priest from entering that most sacred place, the holy of holies.

My taper bearer walked to the menorah. One by one he alternately lit each of the seven candles in the candelabra beginning from the outside. With the help of my other assistants, I tipped the censer and poured the mixture of burning charcoal, frankincense, and oil into the golden vessel that sat on the acacia-wood altar.

Then one by one, I added the sweet spices and gums, the *stacei* myrrh resin, *onycha* powder, and *galbanum* plant resin from three pouches carried by my assistants, spooning, measure by measure, on the lit aromatic substances. As the organics burned, they emitted an appealing fragrance—a sweet smell that rose majestically to our God in heaven. I dismissed my assistants.

As I stood alone before Jehovah, my heart knew that my prayers and the prayers of the congregation standing outside were being honored by our great God. However, one prayer that I had prayed time and time again God seemed to ignore. It was a very special and private prayer.

And then it happened!

Standing suddenly at the right side of the altar was a man; no, more than a man. He had *radiance* about him; even—it seemed—a *glow*! I was shocked! And I was afraid. Then this apparition spoke. He said,

> *Don't be afraid, Zechariah! God has heard your prayer. Your wife, Elizabeth, will become pregnant and give you a son. You shall name him John. His birth will be a joy to you and many others. He will be very special—a great man before God—one filled with the Holy Spirit from the time of his birth. He must not drink any wine or strong drink.*
>
> *He will guide many people back to the Lord their God. Your son will go ahead of the Lord and be strong and mighty like the prophet Elijah! He will bring families together and turn the disobedient back to righteousness; he will get the Lord's people ready to accept him.*

I suppose it was because I didn't want to believe that this person standing before me was really an angel that I challenged him.

"How am I supposed to know that you are real and this will happen? I'm an old man, and my wife is old. We're past being able to have children."

That was the wrong thing to have said. The angel didn't like it. He stared forcefully down upon me, and in a voice that dominated the space, he commanded,

> *I am Gabriel. I stand in the presence of God. He sent me to speak to you and tell you this good news.*
>
> *But you have chosen not to believe my message; be sure that what I said will happen in due time! Because you did not believe you will be unable to speak. You will remain silent until the promise of a son comes true.*

Then he disappeared!

It took awhile for me to orient myself. Yes, I was in the holy place. I had seen an apparition; it was over. I had been there a long time—too long—the people must have been wondering what had happened to me. I know I staggered slightly as I walked out of the holy place. I stood at the steps and tried to explain, but—I couldn't speak! No words came!

I covered my mouth and shook my head back and forth. How do you signal that you have seen an angel? I pointed to the sky and put my hands together as in prayer. I waved my hands directing them to leave. As they began to move out of the courts, they must have wondered, *What happened in the holy place?* It became obvious that many believed I had seen a vision, that God had spoken to me. I had, and he had.

I found shelter in my cubicle and changed into my standard priestly attire. Early the next morning I fled home. As I entered and saw my wife, I motioned for a writing slate and scribbled, "I've seen an angel!"

It was horrible! I couldn't talk. I couldn't tell what had happened to me. I did, however, describe as best I could through motions and writing that an angel had appeared to me with an astounding message. Elizabeth was entirely supportive. She loved me and showed it wonderfully.

LUKE 1:5–23

THEN JACOB SAID

You have probably never heard of me. Most people haven't. I am Jacob, son of Matthan and father of Joseph. I am a Jew and a member of the tribe of Judah. My family tree can be traced all the way back from Abraham to Isaac, Jacob, Judah, Boaz, Jesse, David, Solomon, Rehoboam, Hezekiah, and more.

Ours is a family of patriarchs, and since our

tribal heritage includes the household of King David, a royal family, it is a proud heritage. But, I must add, we are in reality no better than those whose ancestry is traced back through the other eleven tribes.

My wife, Hannah, is also of the tribe of Judah. She had been married previous to our union. Her first husband was my older half brother, Heli. He died while still young, leaving Hannah with no children. Then I, acting in accordance with the command of Moses in the Torah, took Hannah as my wife. Joseph was our firstborn. The records show Joseph as my natural son but Heli as the legal father.

As I said before, you probably have never heard of me. So let me reiterate my status; my *claim to fame* is this: I have the divine privilege of being the grandfather of Jesus of Nazareth. Let me tell you how it happened.

Our son, Joseph, following *in my footsteps*, had grown into a skilled carpenter. He would often say, "If it's made of wood, I can build it." And what he built was of high quality. Joseph had reached the age when marriage became an interest. Our Jehovah wants his men to marry and raise children to his honor.

One day while we were working in the shop,

he commented, "Father, I have been giving much thought to marriage. I believe I am able to support a wife and family. I have enough money saved to build a house. I think it's time for you to select a wife for me."

I understood his real meaning: "Father, it is time for you to choose for me the woman I have already decided I want to marry." He gingerly began to make reference to a young woman who lived at the far end of town. Her name was Mary, the daughter of Joachim and Anne. I had seen her often and on occasion had talked with her. And I knew her parents well.

"I've known Mary pretty much all my life," he observed. "We've played games, sung together at parties, and danced at weddings. She has a handsome face, Father. And she loves to laugh! Every time I've been around her, I've found her to be generous and kind. I think she would make a perfect wife for me."

That evening I talked the matter over with Hannah. She was ecstatic. She and Mary's mother were close friends. And Mary's parents were also of the tribe of Judah and descendents of King David. It would make a perfect match.

The next step was approaching Mary's parents to discuss possible conditions and arrangements. As I walked over to the house of Joachim, I thought about how best to introduce the topic.

A straightforward proposal seemed proper when approaching friends. So after greetings and small talk, I proposed, "Joachim and Anne, we have known each other for many years. We have prayed together, laughed together, even cried together. I am proposing to you today that we be united in yet another way, an even closer way. I propose to you that you agree to give your daughter, Mary, to my son, Joseph, as his wife in holy matrimony."

Joachim and Anne stood up and tried to look aghast! Joachim blustered, "You make a very serious request of us, Jacob. Mary is the jewel of our life. To give her to another family is something that requires considerable thought. Although we are honored by your proposal, you will understand that we need time to consider all that it implies. And we need time to talk with Mary. I as a caring father could not support your proposal unless Mary also agreed to it."

My response supported their position. "I am in full agreement, Joachim. Take time and let me know when we should talk again." And so the visit ended amicably.

I suspected that there had been considerable conspiracy fostered by Joseph and Mary. Joseph betrayed no lack of faith regarding Mary's response to my proposal. Exactly seven days later I was called to receive my answer from Mary's parents.

Joachim's obvious pleasure shone as he stated

quite firmly, "Jacob, I have decided that a contractual arrangement of betrothal should be drawn up between us just as soon as we can agree on the dowry."

It took only two meetings for us to agree on what the dowry should be; it would be a cupboard, table, and stools built by Joseph for Mary's parents.

The engagement contract was drawn up as the day of their betrothal approached. We fathers agreed the rite should happen in the synagogue, since both of us wanted to assure God's blessing on this marriage.

Mary was seated on a bench. Joseph was led to sit beside her. Under the guidance of the rabbi, a formal benediction was spoken over the couple by us, their four parents. Now they were bound together in a covenant between our two families. The event was sealed with a cup of wine and the rabbi's blessing. Everyone left happy.

MATTHEW 1:1–17;
LUKE 3:23–38;
DEUTERONOMY 25:5–10;
MATTHEW 1:18A

THEN MARY SAID

*I*t was just an ordinary day—nothing special. I was in the house sewing. Father was at work, and Mother had gone to market. As often happened these days when I was alone, my thoughts turned to Joseph, about us becoming husband and wife. What would it be like? I knew he was a good man. But living in the same house day after day—eating together—sleeping together—making love; it was overwhelming!

My mind switched to thoughts of God and the women he championed. Women like Deborah, Ruth, and Esther. And I thought about my own life, how I tried to be the woman God wanted me to be, how I tried to obey his laws. I knew that even though I failed him, he loved me and forgave me.

But I yearned for the day when he would send the Messiah. And I remembered that as a young girl I sometimes fantasized how it would be if I were chosen to become the mother of this Anointed One, the mother of the King of the Jews—but those were childish thoughts.

Yes, it was just an ordinary day—until: suddenly, out of nowhere he came, this person—this apparition! He looked like a man, yet—not really. He had radiance about him; even—it seemed—a glow! And he stood there just for a moment. Then he spoke,

Hello, Mary. God's peace is with you.

His voice was calm and deliberate—and assuring.

You are special, Mary. God is very pleased

*with you. You are a blessed woman. God has
chosen you—yes, you, Mary.*

For a moment I was frozen. Was I dreaming?
Was this real? What was happening to me? And his
greeting—what was that all about? I—am special?
God is pleased with me? I'm blessed? I'm a chosen
one? Chosen for what?

Then this man—this apparition—he called
himself the angel Gabriel—continued, assuring
me. He said,

*Don't be afraid, Mary. You have found
favor with God. This is what will happen to
you: you will become pregnant and have a baby.
It will be a boy. You will name him Jesus. He
will be great, and he will be called the Son of
the Highest; and your God, Jehovah, will make
him King like his ancestor David. And this Jesus
will reign over the house of Jacob forever; and
this kingdom of Israel will never end.*

You can imagine what was going through my
mind. Me? A virgin! Being pregnant? I was not
highly versed regarding sex and pregnancy, but
even I knew that pregnancy without sexual intercourse was impossible. Was he kidding? Was this
some kind of a cruel joke?

So I asked, "How can this be true? I've never had sex with a man. I am faithfully waiting until my betrothal to Joseph will culminate in a formal wedding. Only then will I open myself to a man and only one man, my beloved Joseph."

He seemed to have anticipated my response— this Gabriel. He spoke very deliberately to me as he said,

> *Mary, the Holy Spirit of our Jehovah God will come down upon you. You will be impregnated by God. God will be the father of your child; therefore, that baby, that Holy One who is to be born, will be called the Son of God. You will be the mother; Jehovah will be the father.*

Then he went on to say,

> *Your cousin Elizabeth, who was considered to be barren, has conceived, even though she is old. She is even now six months pregnant. She will have a son. You see, Mary, with God nothing is impossible.*

What was I to do? What was I to say? What I saw and heard was real. It had to be. This apparition was real. He truly was an angel. And, unbelievable as it seemed, God had chosen me; God honored me to be the mother of our Messiah King!

And so I stammered, "I am God's handmaiden. Let it happen to me as you have said. Let me become pregnant. Let me be the mother of the one who is called the Son of God."

And then he was gone.

A very short time later my mother, Anne, returned from the market. I tried to pretend that nothing had happened, but it was hard. I must have looked shaken. I remember Mother exclaiming, "Mary, child, you look as if you have seen a ghost!"

My stammered reply was, "It's only because I am having my monthly time." Mother wasn't quite sure she should believe me.

She said, "Did you just not have it last week? Maybe we should see our friend, Eva. She is, you know, more than just a midwife. She will know about these things. She can help."

Trying to hide my anxiety as best I could, I replied, "Mother, I'm sure it will stop soon. If the problem is still with me tomorrow, we can visit Eva."

And with that the matter was dropped.

What should I do? The next several days went on

as usual for the family, but not for me. How could they? The angel had said I would become pregnant. And that God would do it. That's impossible! The angel said that with God nothing is impossible. And the angel said Elizabeth would have a baby, even though she was very old. That may not be impossible, but it surely is improbable. What should I do?

I decided I would wait. I would wait until it was time for my monthly period. Then I would decide.

The next weeks were impossible for me. I prayed and prayed. I asked God to give me a clear vision of what I should do if I was truly pregnant. When my monthly time came, nothing happened! I waited. Perhaps I was just late. Days passed and nothing happened! A week passed; two weeks! I prayed, "Oh, Lord, was the angel real? Am I really pregnant?" My body began to feel different. Each morning when I awoke I felt nauseated. My breasts began to swell!

Now I knew it. It was true. I had no choice. I had to believe that I was pregnant! And so I prayed, "Oh, Lord, help me! Help your humble servant. I don't know what to do. I don't know whom to tell. I can't tell my parents. I can't tell my rabbi. I can't even tell my friends. And I certainly can't tell Joseph. What, oh, Lord, can I do?"

Gradually it came to me. I knew what I must

do. I must get away. Get away before I showed. My Uncle Zeb was a trader. He carried goods between Galilee and Judea. His trader entourage was quite large, about six men leading twenty donkeys and five camels.

I heard that he was leaving within the week for Jerusalem and would pass by Ein Karem, a town southwest of the Holy City. That's where Zechariah and Elizabeth lived. This was providential! I would see for myself if the angel's message about my cousin being pregnant was really true. If Elizabeth was with child, all my doubts would vanish. And I felt that I really needed that final assurance. Only then could I face the world with honor.

Convincing my parents to let me journey to Ein Karem wasn't easy. Father was definitely against it. But Mother knew something very serious was bothering me. She could tell I was definitely distraught. Often they would find me crying. It appeared to them that I was beginning to enter into a deep depression. Not knowing what to think was the cause, Mother chose to assume it had to do with the upcoming wedding. She was aware that I had stopped making preparations. Perhaps a *change of scenery* might help. Elizabeth was the wife of an honored priest. Perhaps their counsel would settle me down.

I heard her say to Father, "Joachim, you need to reconsider your decision about Mary taking a trip to visit our relatives, Zechariah and Elizabeth. They are good people. I believe they can help Mary. We can't simply ignore her condition. She needs counsel. My cousin may be the one who can help."

The next day Father relented. "Anne, you may be right. We should let her go."

I was overjoyed and relieved. I would be going to Ein Karem. I hugged my Father and thanked him with all my heart. Later that day, Father talked with Joseph, and Joseph, being a kind and understanding man, agreed that a short visit with relatives would be good for me; I would be with an honored priest and his wife.

I truly had a loving family and caring husband-to-be, but I didn't dare share my secret. It would have devastated them and brought shame upon them. I was not willing to do that; at least not yet.

And so I prepared myself for the journey. I would be safe with Uncle Zeb as my protector. I knew it would be hard. There would be a lot of walking, eating at camps, and sleeping under the stars. But I was a young, healthy, Hebrew woman. I could do it. We left early morning on the day after Sabbath.

LUKE 1:26–39A

THEN ELIZABETH SAID

O ne of Zeb's men stopped by to tell me that later today I would have a visitor, my second cousin Mary. How happy that made me feel!

You see, following my pregnancy, I hid myself. I couldn't face people. It was just recently that I had been able to force myself to leave the house. Yesterday was my first walk into the marketplace.

I found it difficult to be with people I didn't know well. I saw them look at me and turn away. I knew they were talking about me, about this grey-haired woman from down the street who was pregnant.

And we were, by some, the butt of jokes. "Have you heard about the old geezer and his wife? You'd think they were ready for the grave, at least ready for canes and crutches. But guess what? The old man had more zip than you think; he can still *do the trick.* He got his old lady pregnant. Can you believe it? How in the world did he manage that? Maybe a priest does have special powers. Maybe I should go to synagogue and get some of what he dishes out."

It would be so nice to have a friend, a confidante, someone to share what I had learned about God, about the angel, about becoming pregnant, about whom this son of mine would become. I had so much to tell!

Then Mary arrived. I certainly didn't expect what I saw, or what happened. In came Mary—just beginning to show! Mary was pregnant! She pushed open the door and ran to me.

"Elizabeth!" she cried. "Oh, Cousin, I need you. I'm pregnant! I need you to tell me what to do!" And she hugged me and sobbed. "Elizabeth, I need you. Please help me! Please help me!"

As I hugged her back, I felt a sensation inside of me. My baby seemed to leap inside my womb.

In a barely audible voice, Mary cried to me, "Elizabeth, I had a vision of the angel Gabriel. He told me that God would make me pregnant. And I am! He said that because my baby's father is Jehovah, my child will be called the Son of God."

Then suddenly Mary raised her head from my shoulder and enthusiastically announced, "And he said that you were pregnant. And you are! Oh, Cousin, I am so happy to see you. I'm so happy that you are *really* pregnant. Now I know for sure that what the angel said came directly from God. I am truly blessed."

I was overwhelmed. Slowly I began to realize the impact of what Zechariah had written for me to read after I became pregnant; about the angel appearing to him in the Jerusalem temple; about us becoming parents; about how this son of ours would be filled with the Holy Spirit from the time of his birth; how he, like the prophet Elijah, would be the one to prepare God's people for the soon-to-come Messiah.

And I burst out with joy and proclaimed to Mary, "Child, you are the most blessed of all women! And your baby is blessed! I can't express how fortunate I feel to know that the mother of my Lord came all the way from Nazareth to be with me. When you came into the room, Mary, and hugged me, I could feel my baby jump inside of me. How truly blessed we are. And I can see, Mary, how happy you are, now that you know that what the angel said to you will really come true. This is a time for joy!"

When Zechariah came home, we told him everything that had happened during the day. He listened in amazement. His eyes lit up, and a knowing smile came across his face as Mary detailed her angel visit. I could tell that he was thinking about how similar Gabriel's message to Mary was to the one he had received.

Now, finally he could begin to comprehend the full impact of the events that had begun in the Jerusalem temple. As he connected the two visions, he realized how his revelation intertwined with Mary's vision. With a conviction I seldom saw in Zechariah, he found his writing slate and scribbled as fast as he could:

EACH FAMILY—A CHILD.
OLDER PREPARES FOR YOUNGER.
YOUNGER—PROMISED MESSIAH.

Ours was a jubilant house. We talked, we sang, we prayed. I reminisced about earlier times when my cousin Anne and I had been young and looking forward to becoming brides.

"I remember how lucky I felt when I learned that a marriage contract was being arranged between Zechariah's and my parents. After all, to marry a young priest was an honor. As you know, Zechariah and I both belonged to the house of Aaron of the tribe of Levi. Zechariah's father, Barach, and my father's negotiations were settled in just a few days.

"That was not at all like that of my father's marriage. When Father asked my grandfather to arrange a contract with my mother's parents, there was trouble. You see, while my father was of the tribe of Levi, my mother belonged to the tribe of Judah.

"Families almost never arranged marriages outside their own tribe. Negotiations for those marriage contracts took a long time. It was over two months before permission was granted and details were completed and approved by the elders of our synagogue. But finally, the contract was arranged, and my parents were allowed to marry.

"So, since my father is a Levite and a descendent of Aaron, I am also."

Mary shared the joy she had felt when she had learned that the young man she had admired from a distance would soon become her husband. But, of course, all this was now a complicated conundrum.

Mary was pregnant. No one in Nazareth knew. I feared what would happen to poor Mary when she returned.

One day Mary approached Zechariah and me with a parchment. Mary said, "I have been thinking about all the miracles God has surrounded us with and have written down some thoughts about what has happened."

Then she recited this beautiful poem:

My heart praises the Lord;
My soul is glad because of God my Savior,
For he has remembered me, his lowly servant!
From now on all people will call me happy,
Because of the great things the
Mighty God has done for me;

From one generation to another
He shows mercy to those who honor him.
He has stretched out his mighty arm
And scattered the proud with all their plans.
He has brought down mighty
Kings from their thrones,
And lifted up the lowly.
He has filled the hungry with good things,
And sent the rich away with empty hands.

He has kept the promise he made
to our ancestors,
And has come to the help of his servant Israel.
He has remembered to show mercy
to Abraham
And to all his descendants forever!

(Luke 1:46–55)

We were so proud of Mary. This young girl had been able not only to cope with an unbelievable situation but also to understand it as God's action and herself as God's chosen instrument to make it happen. Now she had ritualized it with this poem. God would surely show Mary his way upon her return to Nazareth.

LUKE 1:24–25; LUKE 1:39–56

THEN ZECHARIAH SAID

*M*ary had been with us for just under three months when one of Zeb's men stopped by to tell us that the caravan was on its way to Jerusalem and would return to Ein Karem in four days on the trip back to Nazareth. The man reported that Zeb had been instructed to take Mary with him.

He returned on schedule. We invited Zeb and

his caravan to stay the night. We had a large house built around a central patio. There was room for all. When it was announced that Zeb had arrived, Mary hid herself. At first it was difficult for all. I couldn't speak, so after a generous hug, I motioned that Elizabeth should talk. She explained that I was temporarily not able to speak and Mary was unavailable; she would necessarily need to speak on my behalf. Being an educated woman, that was no challenge.

She directed, "But before we talk, you should tend to your animals. I will prepare water for you and your men to wash. Then we will eat."

It was, to say the least, an unusual meal with Mary absent and me totally silent. But my dear wife *carried the day* with interesting small talk that occupied the interest of both Zeb and his men.

That evening after dinner, Zeb, Elizabeth, and I, with my motions and nods, had a very private conversation about Mary. Elizabeth shared every detail from the past nine months to the present: my visit from Gabriel, Elizabeth's pregnancy, Mary's visit from Gabriel, and Mary's pregnancy. She tried to show him how this all fit into God's pattern, God's plan for us and for Mary.

Zeb's final comment was, "Elizabeth, I have heard many strange stories in my lifetime, but this one has to be the most bizarre of any so far. Yet, my honorable cousin, I know you to be honest and levelheaded, and I know you are no fool. I will respect your story, and I will honor Mary's pregnancy. Let others be those who scorn. If as you say this is God's work, time will validate your story. God's will be done."

Now Mary was invited to join us. For a time Zeb was quiet as he looked upon her protruding belly.

Then he said, "Peace be with you, Mary. I will carry you safely home to your parents and to Joseph. May God be by your side."

They left early the next morning. Mary was happy to return home, but we could tell she was anxious about the events that would follow. I couldn't blame her. She knew *hers* was God's pregnancy, but who would believe her? I'm sure she felt that her family would feel shamed, not to mention how the village would react. And Joseph—what could she tell Joseph to convince him that she had been faithful—that this was God's doing?

As she hugged and kissed us goodbye, she whispered, "Pray for me. I know I am God's handmaiden in all of this. Pray that all things happen as he directs. Pray that I, Joseph, and my baby will have a contented life."

Then she mounted a donkey Zeb had freed from baggage, and they were off.

Time passed quickly for me, but not for my dear Elizabeth. Being pregnant as a young woman is hard, but pregnancy as an old woman is nearly unbearable. Often at night I heard her groan, and sometimes a barely audible scream would sound from her aching body. Yet, she was joyful knowing that soon she would be a mother, the mother of a chosen child, God's messenger child.

We did not expect such an easy delivery. Praise God! It was all over in just one hour! The baby was healthy—it had ten fingers and ten toes; it even had a crop of red hair on top of its head! What joy! And for me, what pleasure to see Elizabeth nursing our child as he snuggled to her breast and cooed. I hadn't felt joy like this, ever! I was a father. Praise God! All our friends and neighbors rejoiced with us when they heard about the healthy birth.

The eighth day arrived, the day on which all Jewish male children are circumcised. The sacred ritual would take place in our home. Rabbi Hosea arrived. Elizabeth sat in a chair holding our son. Friends had arrived and took seats. Soon the *bris* would begin.

Rabbi Hosea called out the first direction, "*kvatter*." Elizabeth now handed the child to the *kvatterin*, her dear friend Esther, who had agreed to be the child's godmother. As Esther arose and placed the baby into the hands of the *kvatter*, Esther's husband, Ezekiel, the people recited in unison, "May he who comes be blessed." In a final passing of the child, Ezekiel handed our baby to the *mohel*, Rabbi Hosea.

As the rabbi began to spoon a drop of wine to the lips of our son to ease the pain, I rose in protest and held the rabbi's arm. I violently shook my head side to side.

Elizabeth interceded, "Rabbi, our son will never taste of wine or strong drink! We intend to raise him a Nazarite!"

On hearing those words of promise, the rabbi readily relented. "In that case," he whispered, "no wine for him. He will need to learn pain."

Following an intercession and recitation of the prayer, "Blessed are you, our Lord God, Ruler of the universe, who has sanctified us with your commandment and commanded us concerning the rite of circumcision," the act of circumcision was performed.

As a healthy bellow of defiance erupted from the child, the rabbi, speaking for me in my muteness, introduced the conclusion to the ritual with this blessing, "Praised by you, O Lord our God, King of the universe, who has sanctified us by your commandments and has bidden us to make him enter into the covenant of Abraham our father."

The people responded with, "As he has entered

into the covenant, so may he be introduced to the study of Torah, to the wedding canopy, and to good deeds."

Everyone waited. It was now time to name the child. All had assumed that the boy would be named after me. But it was not to be. Elizabeth declared clearly for all to hear, "His name is to be John!"

"What?" The response was negative and universal, "You can't do that. You know our customs. If his name is to have no spiritual significance, he should be named after a family member. There is no relative with that name."

All eyes turned to me. "Zechariah, tell us his name!" I motioned for a writing slate. I was resolute as I wrote; there was but one word, "John!"

And then—praise God! I could speak! Words rolled out of my mouth. I shouted, "Yes, his name is John! It is the will of Almighty God that his name be John! God's angel commanded that his name be John! He will be a Nazarite, but he will be even more. He is the one God has chosen to prepare his people for the coming of their Messiah. Praise God!"

A table had been set up with food and drink. It was a happy time, but for some, a puzzling time.

"What is this child going to be? A Nazarite? But even more? I don't understand."

I chose to wait until after people had eaten. "My friends, please listen to me. You are bewildered, and I don't blame you. Even after all this time, over nine months of searching, I am not sure what the future of our son will be. I only know this. He is chosen for a special role, and the role is related to the coming of our Messiah."

I then went on to say, "Over the last several days I composed a poem to honor this day. I believe that in this poem God's Holy Spirit was speaking to me. I would like to read it to you now. It begins with a statement of praise and a declaration of faith."

Let us praise the Lord, the God of Israel!
He has come to the help of his people
And has set them free.
He has provided for us a mighty Savior,
A descendant of his servant David.
He promised through his holy prophets long ago
That he would save us from our enemies,
From the power of all those who hate us.
He said he would show mercy to our ancestors
And remember his sacred covenant.
With a solemn oath to our ancestor Abraham
He promised to rescue us from our enemies
And allow us to serve him without fear

So that we might be holy and righteous
before him
All the days of our life.

"I then found myself being led to write the following about our son, John."

You, my child, will be called
A prophet of the Most High God.
You will go ahead of the Lord
To prepare his road for him,
To tell his people that they will be saved
By having their sins forgiven.

"I ended my poem with this tribute to Jehovah:"

Our God is merciful and tender.
He will cause the bright dawn
Of salvation to rise on us.
It will shine from heaven on
All those who live in the
Dark shadow of death.
It will guide our steps
Into the path of peace. (Luke 1:68–79)

There was no question; the people were impressed. They wondered, *What does all this mean? What is this child going to be?* It wasn't long before it seemed all of Judea was talking about the circumcision.

It's strange how truth becomes story and story becomes rumor. Our reputation was now that of the old priest who got his old wife pregnant and then lost his voice; he got it back when they had a son who could never drink alcohol.

LUKE 1:57–80

THEN JOSEPH SAID

I am Joseph of Nazareth, a member of the tribe of Judah. My father is Jacob of Matthan. He married my mother after her first husband died. That marriage produced no children.

According to the Torah, if a woman is widowed with no male children, a near relative such as a brother or cousin is to take the widow as his wife so there might be offspring who could rightfully claim the family inheritance. Heli was my mother's first husband.

Therefore, I am the natural son of Jacob and the legal son of Heli. Both Jacob and Heli trace their ancestry to Judah and King David.

Most people consider me to be a good man. I try to be. I am a carpenter by trade. I make farm implements, tables, chairs, tools—in fact, if you need it, I can probably build it. And I do good work.

Until that fateful day, my life was normal. I grew up, learned the carpentry trade, and planned to marry and raise a family who with me would live a simple and honorable life, the life expected of a true son of God. My search to marry stopped abruptly when I met Mary. She lived at the far end of our town, a short walk from my parents' home.

We would meet at local gatherings—parties, weddings, festival days. I found her a pleasing young woman; even more, I found her desirable. I talked with my parents and suggested that I would like them to consider Mary as my future wife. Since I was of that age and Mary's family was an honorable family, my father negotiated with Mary's father to arrange a marriage contract. A day was chosen on which we would pledge ourselves to each other.

It was the most important day for me since my *Bar Mitzvah*. We gathered in the synagogue with her parents, my parents, and friends. The rites were read, the prayers were spoken, and we committed to become husband and wife. Mary was so happy! Now she could begin preparations for the wedding day.

But before that took place, my world was shaken!

That fateful day happened when Mary returned from her visit to Zechariah and Elizabeth. About three months earlier she had insisted that she must visit her relative Elizabeth. She hadn't said why, but I could tell by her insistence that it was very important for her to go. Mary's Uncle Zeb was going up that way, into Judea, and Mary could go along. She would be safe with Zeb and his company of traders. I missed her during these months. And now she was home.

I was stunned! I was humiliated! I was angry! Mary, my Mary, was pregnant! *How could she do that?* She was betrothed to me. Who was the father? How did it happen? Was she an adulteress? Was she raped? How could she humiliate me like that?

What should I do? Should I condemn her before the village? Should I simply release her to her family and her disgrace? Should I do the unthinkable—forgive her and marry her? What would that do to me—to us? Would my business suffer? Would my friends avoid me? What would Jehovah want me to do?

Some days later, after my frustration and anger resided, I met with Mary privately. We talked. I was terribly hurt, but I loved her. As we discussed the situation, Mary told me what seemed like a ridiculously made-up story about an angel appearing to her. She said his name was Gabriel. She insisted that the angel had told her she would become pregnant because the Holy Spirit of God would make her pregnant. The baby would be special, the Son of God, because while she would be the mother, Jehovah would be the father.

She said that while she had believed a real angel had spoken to her back then, she still had some doubt. So she had waited. When her monthly time had not come, she had become more convinced that the angel's words were true.

But, the final verdict would be determined by a visit to Elizabeth. If Elizabeth was also pregnant, as the angel had said, then the rest must be true also. That and her fear of what people would say, what I would say, what I would do, Mary said, was her primary reason for visiting Zechariah and Elizabeth.

This was too much! What was I to believe! Mary's story seemed too preposterous to be true. Yet, Mary had been a virtuous woman. She would not easily lie. But even if I believed her, certainly no one else would. If I accepted her as my wife, we would be an outcast couple. My reputation would be ruined. I would be regarded as having defiled the woman I was supposed to honor. Mary would be regarded as a weak woman, a woman without scruples, even as an adulteress. I needed time to think.

And then it happened. I had had trouble sleeping. My rests were fitful. But one night about a week after my meeting with Mary, I fell into a deep sleep, and the deep sleep turned into a trance. In this stupor I saw standing before me an angel. Perhaps it was Gabriel; I don't know. But I know the dream was real! The angel spoke to me. His voice was calm and convincing.

He said,

Joseph, son of David, do not be afraid to take Mary as your wife, for that which is conceived in her is of the Holy Spirit. And she shall

have a son, and you shall call his name Jesus, for
he will save his people from their sins.

I awoke with a start. At first I could not get my head to clear. I was still in a trance. After some moments I was able to come back to an alert reality. What a revelation! God had sent his angel to quiet all my fears. Mary had told the truth. Now I knew what I must do.

Immediately after breakfast I ran over to Mary's house. We walked to a secluded area, and I shared my dream. I was to be the lawful father of the Messiah King! Together we would raise God's son.

Mary and I were married. There was no party, no festive celebration. Our rabbi performed the rite. Our parents and a few close friends and relatives attended, and that was all. Right after our engagement, I had started to build a house for us. It was now ready. We moved in and began our married life without fanfare. It would remain a platonic relationship until after the child was born.

Later when Mary and I were talking about how God had guided our destinies, we remembered what the holy writer Isaiah had written when he prophesied,

A virgin will become pregnant and have a son, and he will be called Immanuel.

Since we weren't sure about the meaning of *Immanuel*, we asked our rabbi. He told us that *Immanuel* is translated as, "God is with us." That revelation was overwhelming. The baby to be born from Mary was *God with us*; we were in awe.

DEUTERONOMY 25:5–10;
MATTHEW 1:1–17;
LUKE 3:23–38;
APPENDIX PAGE 139–141;
MATTHEW 1:18–25; ISAIAH 7:14

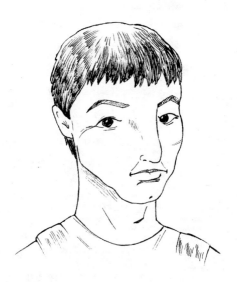

THEN CAESAR SAID

I am Octavian, grandnephew of Julius Caesar and ruler over the Roman Empire. I earned my position after defeating my brother-in-law Mark Anthony following his capitulation to the wiles of the vixen Cleopatra. It was I who brought peace to the empire after one hundred years of civil war. Following that victory the Roman Senate gave

me the name Augustus, appropriately chosen, since it means "the exalted."

I am the one responsible for Rome's honest government; because of me there is sound currency throughout the empire. The extended highway system is my achievement, as is an efficient postal system; I fostered free trade among all parts of my empire. I built innumerable bridges, aqueducts, and buildings adorned with beautiful works of classic art.

I am supreme ruler of a vast empire. My domain stretches as far west as Spain and into northern Britannia. It reaches east to lands beyond the Salt Sea and on to the Caspian Sea; the Danube River marks much of its northern border. Its southern lands include Egypt and most of northern Africa. The Great Sea is my lake. Never before has there been such an extensive and powerful empire.

But even such a glorious empire as mine requires money—lots of money. Therefore, taxes are required. To assure that proper taxes are being collected, it became necessary to order regular censuses. I require Roman citizens to register every fourteen years. The job of compiling information lists necessitates competent men be employed. Census taking is an important job.

Each citizen is carefully evaluated to determine

his riches, rank, and proper place in Roman society. Census counts in the outer regions of my empire are held less often, and the level and focus of scrutiny varies from region to region.

Roman citizens have considered my reign a good time to be alive. Travel and communication have never before been so open and available. Because of me, the world is finally standing on the precipice of a great and glorious future—a time when magnificent things can happen. The gods have so ordained.

LUKE 2:1–3

THEN JOSEPH SAID

A t various intervals Caesar Augustus found it necessary to assure that proper taxes were being collected in the outer regions of his empire. The result was an ordered census of the population of Israel. It was for us a comprehensive census. Not only did Caesar want a count of how many there were, he also wanted a count that defined *who* they were. It was decreed that each family should represent itself for census in the town, city, or region that identified its ancestry at the time of the first kingdom.

For us that meant we needed to follow our ancestry to the time of our first king, Saul. Our family, therefore, was identified with David, who later became King David. We were required to go to David's town, Bethlehem.

Our families discussed how best to meet this census mandate. The decree allowed that legal papers could be submitted by family members who were not able to make the journey to identify their status. So all that was required was that one family member appear and submit the detailed data.

As you may have guessed, the Nazareth community did not hold much respect for either me or Mary. Some thought that I was the guilty party, that I had gotten her pregnant either shortly before or after our engagement.

There was a lot of gossip going around. "It's too bad. Here we thought Joseph an honorable man, but look what he did. No good man dishonors his woman before they are legally married. And you would think that Mary could have said no. It's a shame."

Others thought her pregnancy had happened while she'd been in Ein Karem. "It's amazing what a girl will do when she is away from the eyes of her parents and her community. Did she honestly think she could play the harlot and not get caught? The shame! A *bastard* child! Shame!"

A few thought that perhaps she had been raped by one of Zeb's men while en route. "It's as I always said. These caravan men, they'll find a way to get a girl to lift her skirt. Mark my word; they have their ways with women. If worse comes to worse, get 'em alone and scare 'em into it."

In any case, Mary was suspect, I was suspect, and people avoided us.

Mary and I talked the matter over. Should we volunteer to be the delegates? Although I didn't tell the families, I was looking for an escape from Nazareth. I needed a new start. Better to live in Bethlehem where no one knew the circumstances of Mary's pregnancy than live here under continual scorn. I could take my trade anywhere. Better to be a new but respected carpenter in David's town, than an established but despised carpenter in my hometown.

So, I approached my father and told him, "I've been thinking about relocating, Father. My first choice had been Sepphoris. It's an energetic and growing community. And it's less than a first hour's morning walk northwest of us. I could easily find new work, and we would be away from the accusing eyes of our community.

"But I've changed my mind. Now that the Bethlehem problem is upon us, perhaps a temporary relocation to David's town might be the better choice. Mary and I can represent our two families for the census. We could find a house in Bethlehem and wait for the baby to arrive. I realize that for Mary this trip will be difficult, but her pregnancy is going well. If we leave immediately after the Sabbath, we should arrive in Jerusalem shortly after the next Sabbath. The trip will be long for Mary, but if she rides our donkey, it will make the journey bearable. We'll travel slowly, resting often."

Father's concern was expressed as, "How will you provide? How will you support your family?"

"I'm not concerned, Father; I can provide. There's always work for a skilled carpenter. And then, after Mary and the baby have had sufficient time to recover, we will return to Nazareth; and hopefully, the criticisms will have stopped, and life can go back to normal."

It was settled. Father agreed. We would leave as soon as I finished a couple of jobs.

Bethlehem is about five to seven days south of us. We could take the more direct route across the Samaritan hills, or we could follow along the Jordan River valley to Jericho and then climb west up the Wilderness Road to Jerusalem. From there it would be about a half day's journey south to Bethlehem. If we spent the night in Jerusalem and left early the next morning, we would easily be in David's city by midafternoon.

Our departure followed the Sabbath. After hugs, kisses, and tearful blessings, we departed into an unknown future, Mary astride a donkey with a second creature tethered behind, encumbered with clothing and my carpentry tools.

Part of our journey was with the accompaniment of others who were also setting out for their ancestral homes, one person to Abraham's burial town, Hebron; another to Jericho, where the walls *came tumbling down* at God's command; and a couple from the Manasseh tribe to Beit Shean, gruesomely famous because King Saul's body was hung there after his defeat by the Philistines.

We stayed with the others until Beit Shean, where it seemed we should stop and rest. This Roman town held comfortable accommodations for us. After a full day of rest, we continued alone to Jericho, where we again rested and this time for two full days, one to honor Sabbath.

The most difficult part of our whole journey was the trek up on the mountain road to Jerusalem. Our target was the home of Mary's aged grandparents who lived in the northeast part of the city, not far from the Antonia Fortress that abutted the holy temple. We had to climb from Jericho, resting far below sea level to Mount Moriah rising far above sea level. We left before sunrise and arrived at Mary's grandparents' home in Jerusalem just after sundown. Mary was totally exhausted.

We had a pleasant stay in Jerusalem. Mary's grandparents had no information about the *so-called illegitimate child* in Mary's womb. Together we rejoiced about the immediate future. We had originally planned a single day in Jerusalem. However, it didn't take long to be persuaded to lengthen our stay.

The first full day was a day for rest. We limited our walking with a visit to the nearby Pool of Bethsaida, located just outside the Sheep Gate. It was a large, spring-fed pool separated by a long portico into two distinct areas. We sat at one of the other porticoes and watched as men and women with various infirmities rested near the water.

I asked, "Why are all these pitiful people sitting about the pool?"

"It's very simple," answered Grandfather David, "This pool is called the House of Mercy. There is a tradition that says an angel of the Lord also rests beside these waters. Every so often, say the believers, the angel stirs the waters. The first person to enter the pool once the waters are troubled is healed."

The conversation drifted to Mary's parents. Grandmother Esmerentia reminisced about the *good old days* when Mary's parents had first gotten married. "Your mother and father were quite poor when they married. Since we had this large house, we had them live with us."

Mary blushed when Grandfather inserted with a wink, "You are sleeping in the same room your parents used as their honeymoon bedroom. That's where you were conceived, Mary."

Grandmother, joining in with a smile, reminded, "That is the very bed on which you were born."

Mary asked, "Why did they move to Nazareth, Grandfather?"

"Your Uncle Efran lived just north of Nazareth. He was a stone mason. His business was growing, so he asked your father to join him. Your uncle expected his business to increase since the neighboring town of Sepphoris was growing and supposed by many to have a bright future. Your father decided that a stone-building trade would provide for him and your mother, so they moved.

"And now I hear that Herod Antipas may choose Sepphoris as his Galilean capital city."

The next day, as expected, Mary's grandparents insisted, "You must visit the holy temple. We're so close to it—its right next door—there's nothing more magnificent." And, of course, we agreed.

The holy temple was just as I remembered—but more than Mary could have imagined! I had been there many times with my parents, but for Mary this was a first time.

We entered through the western Coporius Gate into the Court of the Gentiles. I was struck by the noise and activity along the south side of the court. I could see cages holding doves, others holding sheep and goats. Money changers stood in booths ready to convert Caesar's money into temple money. Everywhere, it seemed, men were hawking their products.

Mary's grandfather bristled, "This is sacrilege! The holy temple should be a house of prayer; instead it has become a common market. And, I'm afraid, it will stay this way. Most of these kiosks are owned by the high priest's family. It's a big moneymaker."

We next passed into the Women's Court. All Jews—and only Jews—were permitted admission into this court. It was a happy place where we could see Jehovah being worshiped with dancing, singing, and musical instruments. Grandfather David and I entered the Court of Israel. Women were not allowed. Here we could see the Court of Priests with its golden sacrificial altar and all that was necessary to support the various sacred rituals.

We looked farther, into the holy place. We could identify tables for showbread, a menorah, and the altar of incense. Beyond those hung a large curtain to separate all from the most holy of holies, where once Moses' Ten Commandment tablets, Aaron's staff, and a container of manna had been entombed inside the holy ark of the covenant, a chest with angelic forms hovering above. This was Jehovah's earthy abode.

After returning to the Women's Court, Grandfather reminded us of something we had not thought about, "After the child is born, and after the appropriate time, you should come back to Jerusalem. We would be so pleased if you let us be part of Mary's purification rite and if our great grandchild is a boy, the redemption rite. Why, it could all take place right here in the temple. Just think, Mary, you and your child could be blessed on this holy ground."

We left for Bethlehem early the next morning. The sun was bright and the day warm. It was an easy road, no hills to climb. As we passed Rachel's tomb, we were both reminded of what risks there are with bearing a child, how Rachel had died while giving birth to Benjamin.

My silent prayer was, "Lord, don't let me experience the sorrow of Jacob. Keep Mary safe as she delivers this child."

We arrived in Bethlehem midafternoon. I immediately sought a place to stay. Perhaps I should have anticipated, but I found that the only inn had all of its rooms rented, most of them long-term.

Reason should have told me that Bethlehem would be bustling.

I angrily reminded myself, *You should have known better. You should have realized that the place would be overridden with David's people. Just think. How many wives did David have? How many children did David have? Of course, there would be multitudes who traced their ancestry back to the king.*

What was I to do? We had to have accommodations. I found that some people were staying in the several caves that surrounded the town. I asked about.

A considerate woman tried to help, "These caves are quite acceptable as temporary quarters. They are a cross between a stable and a house. You have to cook outside, but there is considerable space to lie down inside. If you're a city person, you may not find the company of animals to your liking, but in general, they don't bother; and you won't be chilled because their bodies generate considerable heat."

An hour before sundown, I found a stable/house cave that was still available. The owner charged a modest rent. Now we had a place to stay, and there was plenty of straw available. Mary slept well that night. The next morning we walked to the market in search of food. After breakfast I returned to the inn. Still there was no room. I looked for a house to rent. No luck. Even though I continued to search daily, there was no other accommodation available. Our stable/house cave would become our home for the next two weeks.

Our baby would be born in the stable.

LUKE 2:1–5

THEN MARY SAID

I spent most of the day resting. It was true; the heat generated by the animals did keep the cave comfortable at night. I wondered, *When will my baby boy be born? I am ready. I feel good.* I prayed often, "Dear Lord, please give me a healthy baby and an easy delivery." I knew God was listening.

It was just past sundown. I could feel the pains

begin. I called to Joseph, who was tending the fire outside.

He ran to me and asked, "What is wrong? What should I do?"

There was little he could do. I would have to do this all by myself. But I needed him. I had no midwife, no one to guide the birth. And I'd never done it before! I had been present when other babies had been born, however, and I remembered. I could do this!

I pleaded, "Joseph, help me up so I can reach the rails on the pen."

He gently raised me. I grabbed a wooden rail and hung on with all my strength. "Joseph," I cried, "let me alone now. Let me have my baby!" He looked pleadingly into my eyes and then left me to do what only I could do.

The pains became fiercer. My urge to push became ever stronger—irresistible! With a loud scream, I pushed and pushed—the baby dropped to the clean straw below.

I cried out, "Joseph, come quickly! The baby's out! As he ran to me, I grunted, "Take the baby and clean him." Soon I was empty. "Joseph, help me wrap him in these birthing cloths and then take away the mess I've created! I want to hold my baby."

There is no greater joy than nursing the one you held inside you for nine months, your own flesh and blood. I lay on the straw with Joseph at my side, totally content. Joseph had prepared an empty manger to act as a cradle for our son. He lifted the boy and laid him on the soft straw he had strewn throughout the manger.

Our baby was soundly sleeping. I was also about to fall asleep when noise invaded our cave. Some strange men entered; ever so politely they entered. They asked, "Is this the child who is to be our Savior, our Christ the King?"

That question shocked me back to the reality of the past months—our engagement, the angel Gabriel, pregnant without intercourse, Zechariah's vision, Elizabeth's pregnancy, Joseph's dream, our marriage, and now this question, "our Savior, our Christ the King?"

The men introduced themselves as local shepherds. They had a flock down in the valley in what some called the shepherds' field. It was a location that had a sheepfold, water supply, and watering trough, a welcome place to keep sheep overnight.

One of the shepherds—he seemed to be the leader—told this astounding story:

"We were, as usual, camped next to our flock, all resting near the water trough. It was a pleasant and quiet night. Eli was playing the flute, and some of us were singing. Then suddenly, out of nowhere, he came! An angel—an angel of the Lord appeared in the sky! He had radiance—a glow! We were scared as we've never been scared before! But the angel said to us,

> *Don't be afraid. I have good news for you. A great joy will come to all people! Today, in David's town your Savior was born—Christ the Lord! And this is what will prove it to you: you will find a baby wrapped in birthing cloths and lying in a manger.*

In utter amazement I began to wonder, *What does this all mean? Shepherds coming, an angel appearing—something is happening—more than I know.*

Another shepherd continued, "Then, after the first angel finished talking, a whole multitude of angels suddenly appeared in the sky above us. And they started to sing! It was the most beautiful song I have ever heard! I can still hear them,

> *Glory to God in the highest heaven, and peace on earth to those with whom he is pleased!*

And then they were gone!"

Another chimed his elation, "We stood for a long while as if in a trance. Then Enos, rather

enthusiastically I must say, demanded, 'Brothers, let's go right now to Bethlehem, and let's see this thing that has happened! Let's see for ourselves what the angel said happened!' And so we are here—could we please see the baby now?"

The shepherd leader looked dutifully at the child and bowed his head in prayer. Others followed suit. They were worshipping our baby! Joseph and I looked at each other in amazement.

They left, quietly, but once they were out of sight, I could hear them shouting, singing, and praising God. The next day neighbors came by to see. Many said they had come because some shepherds had told them a fantastic yet marvelous story about some angels and our son. They were amazed at the enthusiasm of these men.

I couldn't grasp it all; it was too much. *What does all this mean? Could it be true that my baby is the promised Joshua—the Jesus—the Savior? Will he be the Messiah—the Christ—the Anointed One? Is this what Gabriel meant?*

I hid these thoughts deep within my heart. It was too early to know.

LUKE 2:6–20

THEN JOSEPH SAID

*I*t took some intensive searching, but when our child was four days old, I finally found a house to rent. We moved in and set up housekeeping. What a relief to be out of the cave and away from the animals! Mary's time was occupied with meals, washing, cleaning, and of course tending to the many demands of our baby.

The Lord again supplied our needs. The day

after we moved, I was asked if I would build a bed and cabinet for our new neighbor. His family had grown, and he needed more sleeping space. It was good to be working and providing.

As commanded in the Torah, when our son was eight days old, we took him to the synagogue; our son was to experience circumcision. Jehovah had told our father Abraham some two thousand years previously that all males born to Jewish families must have the foreskin of the penis cut back. Jehovah commanded,

> *You must agree to keep this covenant with me, both you and your offspring. You and all your descendants must agree to circumcise every baby boy among you when he is eight days old.*

The ritual was performed by the local rabbi in accordance with God's command. He was named Jesus, the name given to him by the angel Gabriel.

We continued to live in Bethlehem, and I continued to find work. Life was good. Soon it would be forty days since Mary had given birth. It was time to redeem our son from the Lord and for Mary to complete the ritual of purification. We intended that these acts would take place in the holy temple in Jerusalem. The trip to the Holy City was not difficult. Mary's faithful donkey gladly accepted the added weight of the baby.

Mary's grandparents were happy to see us and ecstatic to see the baby. What a fuss they made! It wasn't long before her Grandmother Esmerentia brought out a colorful crib blanket she had quilted, one in which were stitched images of ducks, donkeys, and sheep.

Grandfather David appeared equally practical, saying, "I noticed when you were here before Jesus was born that among your carpenter tools was a badly worn wood plane with a chipped blade. So with the help of my blacksmith friend, Rueben, and my handyman nephew, Mathias, I was able to figure out a way to build a truly quality plane; one made of solid acacia wood with a stone-sharpened blade. Joseph, may all your newly built tables and cabinets have a surface as smooth as our great grandson's baby skin."

Then it was time to eat. We would visit the holy temple tomorrow.

As we had done before, we and Mary's grandparents again entered the holy temple through the western Coporius Gate, I carrying Jesus with Mary at my side. We walked over to the kiosk area in the

Court of Gentiles where I purchased two doves, one for a burnt offering and one as a sin offering. I asked Mary to carry Jesus, while I did my best to manage the doves. Thankfully the vendor had tied each securely at the feet.

After passing through the Beautiful Gate, we arrived at our destination, the Court of Women. Crossing to an area where several Levites sat in booths, I explained to one that we wished to fulfill obligations for our newly born son and my wife. He ordered, "So that your obligations may be properly recorded, tell me your name and town and your wife and child's names." Upon completion of the formality, we proceeded to an altar area where the rites would be performed.

A priest approached. I again clarified our purpose. The priest led us to one of several altars.

He announced, "I declare the holy Rite of Redemption to begin. Since every firstborn son in a Jewish family was saved when the angel of the Lord passed over his home in Egypt, every firstborn son has belonged to God and to God only. Present your son to the Lord. "

I handed Jesus to the priest. He blessed our son and said, "By this act you have declared that your son is God's own. But God is just and God is kind. I now ask, do you intend to redeem this, your firstborn son?"

My yes was emphatic. The priest continued,

"It is then required that you now offer to God the redemption price, five shekels." I opened my purse and handed five temple shekels to the priest. He in turn handed them to his Levite assistant, who dropped them into the nearest of the thirteen horn-shaped treasury receptacles. After additional ritualized words had been spoken, the rite was complete.

The Rite of Purification began with an invocation and prayers. The priest then said, "Our God declared in the Torah that after a woman has given birth she is unclean. The Rite of Purification will remove her uncleanness and she will be ritually pure. It is now necessary that the child's mother offer to God a purification sacrifice. What have you brought?"

Mary held out our two doves. The priest accepted both birds and gave them to his Levite assistant, who carried them through the Nicanor Gate to the Court of the Priest as offerings to our God. The rite continued with a ritual bath.

Shortly after the priest pronounced a final blessing on Mary, an old man approached us. He spoke softly as he introduced himself. "My name is Simeon. I live in the city. I came to you because God's Holy Spirit led me here. I have been waiting for you for a long time."

I didn't know what to say. He appeared an honest man, even a God-fearing man.

He continued, "I have prayed daily that I might live to see Israel's salvation, the Messiah, and he is here; he is your son."

I was about to move away when Mary interceded, "I trust this man, Joseph, and I believe he has been led by the Holy Spirit for a reason. Trust him."

The old man then asked that he might hold Jesus. I hesitated but finally agreed. After placing our son in the old man's bosom, this Simeon changed; he seemed to move into a trance. He looked up to heaven, and half-crying, half-laughing, he gently shouted,

> *Now, Lord, you have kept your promise, and now you may let your servant go in peace. With my own eyes I have seen your salvation, which you have prepared in the presence of all peoples: a light to reveal your will to the Gentiles and bring glory to your people Israel.*
>
> *(Luke 2:29–32)*

We were awestruck! Simeon gently handed Jesus to his mother. Then he blessed us and tenderly said to Mary,

This child is chosen by God for the destruction and the salvation of many in Israel. He will be a sign from God that many people will speak against and so reveal their secret thoughts. And sorrow, like a sharp sword, will break your own heart.

(Luke 2:34b-35)

Before we could recover, a very old woman descended upon us. She said she was Anna, daughter of the famous Phanuel of the tribe of Asher. Telling us more than we cared to know, she continued, "I was married for seven years when my husband died, and now I've been widowed for eighty-four years. They call me a prophetess. Can you believe it? A prophet! They even awarded me a room in the temple as my home. They are so kind. Their generosity allows me to spend all my days in worship, praying, and fasting."

I had to admit; she was fascinating!

This Anna then prayed, emotionally thanking God for sending our son as a Messiah. We watched as she left. We could see her approaching person upon person and pointing to our son. We left in a hurry, just as the avalanche of people began its descent in our direction.

As we walked from the temple, Mary grasped my arm and said, "Joseph, I am now a purified woman. Until now, you have made no sexual demands upon me. You have been so patient, so kind and understanding. Tonight, Joseph, tonight we will truly share the same bed. Tonight I will give myself to you as your true wife." And so it was.

We arrived at Mary's grandparents' house to find her Uncle Zeb visiting. We immediately bombarded him with questions about the families in Nazareth. "Are the folks okay? And what about the brothers and sisters? Our nieces and nephews? Our friends? Are they expecting us to return to Nazareth soon?" Zeb answered as best as he could.

Then Mary's grandfather shared news we had not expected, "Mary, we are getting very old. As you probably could tell, it's becoming difficult for us to manage by ourselves in this big house. After your last visit, we decided to ask your mother and father if they would live with us and help care for our needs.

"They said yes. Mary, your mother and father are planning to move here. We had not mentioned this before because we were not certain if it would happen. Zeb only brought us the news today."

Mary was elated! "We will be close to both my parents and my grandparents, only a half day's journey away. Praise our loving God!" After two more days of visiting and three nights of celebrating our love, we journeyed back to Bethlehem.

LUKE 2:21–38; GENESIS 17:9–14;
EXODUS 13:1–2, 11–16;
NUMBERS 18:15–16; LEVITICUS 12:1–8

THEN GASPAR SAID

We had been scanning for months, tracking the movements of three planets—Jupiter, Saturn, and Mars. "What do you think, Melchior? What does this mean? Is it possible that these heavenly lights are the signal? Are they the precursor to the promised king we've been researching these many years? Has he finally arrived?"

My name is Gaspar, and I am a priest of the caste of Zoroastrianism. I am one of a faculty of men whose life is devoted to the study of astronomy and its interpretation. Astrological research is a highly developed science in Persia. Tracing the movements of heavenly bodies and offering meaning to these movements occupies most of our time. Ours is a highly respected study. We are called upon by many in high positions to explain how events in the heavens affect what happens on this earth.

A particularly significant study we are associated with relates to a tradition learned from the Hebrews following their relocation into our lands under the ancient King Nebuchadnezzar. The tradition's roots can be found in the Torah where the non-Jew Balaam prophesied,

> *I look into the future, and I see the nation of Israel. A king, like a bright star, will arise in that nation. Like a comet he will come from Israel.*
>
> *(Numbers 24:17a)*

Jewish kings gradually became identified with a star. Over time, the Balaam prophecy grew into a mantra that convinced many to expect that a heavenly light would signal the birth of the Jewish

Messiah. There was an old established belief among many scholars in Persia that fate had decreed a Jewish man to appear who would become the ruler of the world. This tradition also allowed that a star appearing in the sky could set the stage for this king.

Balthazar had, until now, been silent. "The conjunction of Jupiter and Saturn in Pisces is truly a significant event. We've never seen this before. Jupiter is the king's planet."

"And," inserted Melchior, "the ringed planet, Saturn, is the shield and defender of Israel."

"In addition," I alleged, "these planets are in conjunction within the constellation of the Fishes, also associated with Israel."

"But," reminded Melchior, "that has never been enough to convince us this is the true sign of a king. Now, however," he continued, "since a third planet, Mars, has joined the conjunction and with Jupiter and Saturn forms a triangle, I am convinced the time is right." Balthazar and I agreed. It was time to act. We informed our faculty of our findings and conclusions and began plans for a journey to the land of the Israelites. We would see for ourselves if our hypothesis was correct that a king had risen.

Transportation was sought and supplies inventoried. We contracted a caravan that made all the arrangements. It took about a month, but after providing for family needs during our absence, we set out on our trek across some rather challenging country.

Our target was Jerusalem, capital city to the host of Judean kings beginning with David. It took over six weeks to complete the journey, but finally we arrived. After entering the city and finding lodging for our entourage, we began our search. We inquired first among the people. They knew nothing. Thinking that this king would somehow be associated with the Jewish temple, we approached several members of the Sanhedrin. "Do you have any information about a Messiah King?" we asked. "Has anyone come forth with credentials to confirm his arrival?" The answers continued to be negative.

We were advised that if anyone knew about a future king it would be Herod, so we requested an audience with His Highness.

MATTHEW 2:1–2; NUMBERS 24:14–19

THEN HEROD SAID

My chief minister, Zerubabel, approached and bowed, saying, "Your Highness, a party of men who are priests from Persia is here, requesting an audience. What is your wish, sir?"

I wondered out loud, "What could Persians want with me? I have no direct dealings with that

part of the world. Are they a delegation sent by some ambitious tyrant?"

Better not to take chances. "Check them out," I commanded. "Zerubabel, contact my advisors and find out who these men are and what they want."

Uninvited guests needed to know that they approached me only at my pleasure. I would wait for my minister's report.

My name is Herod. I am the king of the Jews. I was appointed to this office by Octavian after his defeat of Anthony earned for him the office of first Caesar of the Roman Empire. He took the name Augustus. Even though I had at first supported Anthony in his fight to gain the throne, I realized my mistake and wisely switched my support to Augustus. He rewarded me with my crown. Apparently I had persuaded him that I would be a capable and trustworthy steward for this Jewish state that lay just east of the Great Sea. I would be his *client king*. And I proved deserving of that trust. I ruled firmly, and I ruled well.

And so I rose from being the appointed governor of Galilee to king of all Israel. My jurisdiction included Judea, Samaria, Galilee, Perea, Decapolis, and regions to the northeast. I ruled a small but strategic state.

Some call me *the Builder*; others call me *the Great*. I am both.

During my reign I built a glistening white seaport city with a hippodrome, an amphitheater, a temple, and a large protected harbor which I named Caesarea Maritima in honor of my emperor. I built the mesa fortress Masada just off the west coast of the Salt Sea. I actually constructed a mountain on which to set my Herodium fortress. I rebuilt Samaria. It was I who put up that huge edifice on top of the Caves of the Patriarchs in Hebron.

I greatly refortified Jerusalem. I constructed a new market, a theater, a Sanhedrin meeting hall, and a fabulous palace in the Holy City.

But the crown jewel of all my efforts is my holy temple; I restored the ancient Temple of Solomon beyond its original glory and protected it with my Antonia Citadel.

In addition, I control the Sanhedrin; I appoint the men to be Jewish high priests. And I am to be feared! I destroyed those who attempted to usurp my authority. Even some in my family were guilty of such treason.

I have absolute power over Israel because I am known as a *friend of Caesar*. This high status plus victories over numerous other enemies of the state demonstrate my supremacy. I am king of the Jews! I am Herod the Great!

Within an hour my chief minister, Zerubabel, stood before me. "Your Highness, the men who request an audience represent a religious group of Zoroastrian priests. They are men of learning, highly proficient in the science of astronomy. They have come here to inquire about a star and a future king."

On hearing the words *future king*, a sharp pang surged through my chest. Hadn't I had enough of would-be kings trying to take my throne? I would see these men.

"Send them in and watch them carefully!"

The priests were resplendently dressed. They obviously were men of wealth and high standing. After submissively approaching my throne, and after appropriate introductions, one of them acted as spokesperson.

"Your Highness, we have traveled for many days, beginning our journey in Persia. Our profession is focused on the study of heavenly bodies, their movements, and the meanings associated with these movements. Our attention was drawn to a conjunction of three of these bodies in particular—Jupiter, Saturn, and Mars, all within the constellation, Pisces. Sir, we believe that what we witnessed is a portent of universal consequence, a precursor of a Messiah King of the Jews.

"We believe that the conjunctional star hails the birth of this future king. You, sir, of all people would know about this, for you are Herod, the great king of the Jews. And we understand that nothing escapes your awareness. So we humbly ask, sir, where is the child that has been born king of the Jews? We wish to know so that we may worship him."

Again, the pang plagued my chest! But I had to appear calm and knowing. I gathered my composure and slowly responded, "I appreciate your coming to me to learn of this momentous event. However, while little escapes my eyes, I do not have direct information regarding this event. These concerns are relegated to my Jewish council, and they report to me. Come back at this time tomorrow, and I will be able to give you a definitive answer."

And with that they were dismissed.

"Send the chief priests and elders to me, immediately. Tell them it is a matter of urgency!" Within the hour I had a collection of my council readily awaiting my bidding. I had commanded Zerubabel to summarize what had transpired with the Zoroastrian priests.

I became somewhat frustrated with the lengthy narrative and interrupted, "Where is this Messiah that the priests talked about to be born?" These church leaders, portraying a false sense of calm, asked for a time to consult.

After a few minutes my chief priest replied, "Your Highness, this Messiah is to be born in the town of Bethlehem in Judea, for the prophet Micah wrote,

> *Bethlehem, in the land of Judah, you are one of the smallest towns in Israel, yet out of you will come a ruler to guide my people. Your family line goes back to ancient times.*

After further clarification I dismissed the assembly and called the visitors from the East for a secret meeting. I needed more information—confidential information.

My only question: "When did the star first appear?"

"Sir," the tall priest replied, "the conjunction of stars began over two years ago. However, it did not resolve into a single image within Pices until eighteen months previous. It was only then that we felt the three bodies could be perceived as one."

It was at this point that my ingenious plan was conceived. I carefully constructed a scenario which persuaded them that I too welcomed this new king. I crafted my words carefully, "I too am looking for the Messiah. I consider myself a caretaker for my

God, Jehovah. My single mission as king has been to hold this land under one leader until it is time to turn it over to the true king, our Messiah King.

"Go," I requested in the most sympathetic of terms. "Make a careful search for the child, and when you find him, let me know, so that I too may go and worship him."

They left, happily anticipating their appearance before the assumed future Messiah King. I learned later that these gullible *wise men of the East* claimed they again saw their star. I was not impressed.

MATTHEW 2:1–10; MICAH 5:2

THEN MARY SAID

We would definitely stay in Bethlehem. Joseph's business was going very well. It had reached a point where he decided to take on an apprentice. The young man named Gideon lived in Bethlehem and was seeking to learn a respectable trade. He proved to be a hard-working, honest young man. Joseph trusted him to such a degree that after a short time he felt quite comfortable leaving the business in his hands if he should need to.

This necessity happened sooner than we had expected. We received word that my mother and father had arrived at my grandparents' home. It was time to ask Gideon to run the business for a while so we could take a trip to Jerusalem.

The journey passed quickly. What a joy to see them, and what a joy for them to see our baby. There was little else that could have cheered my mother as much as holding the baby Jesus and rocking him to sleep. It was hard to leave them and return home; but we were not wealthy, and so our lives demanded that Joseph return to his business.

I was sitting in front of our house, holding my son and preparing some food. In the distance I could hear the din of a boisterous interruption. "What is that noise? Joseph! Who is that coming?"

Approaching our house was a crowd such as I had never seen before. "Joseph, come here!"

At the front of the assemblage was a man leading a camel. Behind were more camels, some laden with goods, and a dozen or more men, three dressed much more luxuriantly than the rest. Behind them paraded a crowd of excited children yelling and laughing, along with a troop of curious adults, both men and women. As they came nearer, the lead man motioned for all to stop. A hush fell over the crowd. He then approached me and bowed.

"Madam," he said, "I am Jabbareh. This is my caravan. I have brought to you three men of great distinction who wish to speak with you." He motioned his men to move the mob away from the house. This was not time for curiosity-seekers to interrupt what he understood would be a very hallowed action on the part of the three men he served. With much pushing and shoving, the crowd was dispersed, and quiet once again dominated the area. By this time Joseph had arrived from the carpentry shop. Jabbareh then asked, "Sir, may I present my masters to you?"

"Yes, let them approach," Joseph answered. The men stepped forward, each dressed in splendid attire. They walked to within a respectful distance and stopped. Each got to his knees and bowed until his forehead touched the ground.

Then one spoke, "Madam and sir, we have come a long way. We are men of learning, men who study the stars for its meaning in our lives. Our investigations revealed a particular star as evidence that a new king is born in Israel. We first traveled to Jerusalem but were informed that this king was to be born not in Jerusalem but rather in Bethlehem. The star led us to your house, madam and sir, and to this child.

"Your son, madam and sir, is the one promised

in your Jewish Scripture, the one Micah prophesied as the king who will arise in Israel, the one
you call Messiah. We are here to worship him and
to offer him gifts."

I was so astounded that I could not speak.
Again, Joseph took control. "Gentlemen and honored guests, please enter our humble abode."

The three splendidly dressed men arose and

politely followed us inside the house. I sat holding Jesus. Joseph stood behind me. The men arranged themselves before us and beside each other and again knelt.

The one who called himself Gaspar uncovered a chest. As he placed the open chest filled with gold before Jesus, he said, "May this young royalty never want and forever be prosperous."

Melchior followed with his chest. "May this priestly frankincense ever be a sweet aroma of praise and thanksgiving rising to your God."

Balthazar offered a third chest containing myrrh. "Dear child, accept this resin, and may you, as did those great prophets of old, stand firm until your earthy mission is complete."

Since there was space behind the carpenter shed, the three men commanded a tent be set up, rugs laid, couches placed, and our family invited to join in a feast. The area was kept clear of prying eyes. Joseph took the gifts into the house and secretly hid them. Because the crowd was kept away from seeing what took place inside our house, none, we hoped, knew that we had received such valuable gifts. But we would have to be careful.

The evening was spent enjoying a meal of lamb with a variety of greens and ample wine. At the appropriate time, Joseph and I, with the sleeping baby in my arms, took leave. The men and their entourage lay in the tent and surrounding grounds. Soon all was quiet. But it was difficult to sleep.

Shortly after sunrise the caravan was gone.

MATTHEW 2:9–11

THEN MELCHIOR SAID

We traveled but a short distance, then stopped and made camp. We needed a day to rest and to resupply our caravan for the journey home. And as pointed out by our caravan leader, "The men need a time to relax and enjoy some night life," little as there was in this town.

I usually sleep well, no bad dreams, no

nightmares, just a good sleep. But this night was different. I had a dream, one like never before. As soon as it was dawn, I roused my startled companions with the message, "Gaspar! Belthazar! I had a powerful dream last night! I saw an angel!"

But before I could continue, each of my companions interrupted with, "So did I!" We shared stories. Each of us had had a vision in which an angel warned us about King Herod. We were told,

Do not return to Herod. He is intensely threatened by your visit. He considers the Bethlehem child a challenge to his throne. And as he has done before when threatened, he will find this Messiah King and kill him.

We returned home using a different route.

MATTHEW 2:12

THEN JOSEPH SAID

We knew that these men from the East were camped just outside town, but we chose not to visit with them. They broke camp the following morning.

We were alone again. I went back to my work building a plow for a local farmer, and Mary tended to her wifely chores. Life was back to normal, or so I thought.

Evening came and all was quiet outside. I fell asleep early. And then it happened—again. Once more I was visited by an angel. I can still see him standing at the side of our bed, looking down on me and saying,

Joseph, listen to me carefully. Herod knows about your child. He knows he was born in Bethlehem. He sees the child as a threat to his throne. He will send soldiers to search for him in order to kill him. Get up now! Take the child and his mother and escape to Egypt. Do not wait! Stay there until I tell you to come back.

I awoke with a start! I shook Mary urging her, "Wake up, Mary. We have to leave. We have to leave tonight! *Now!*" It took a few minutes for my head to clear before I could tell her my dream. Mary listened and thought.

At last she said, "Joseph, we must not ignore this dream. We know that's how God talks with you. Herod is a murderer. If the astronomers told Herod about us yesterday, there could be soldiers coming for our son even now! They could be here by morning. We must not wait. We must do as the angel says and be gone before dawn. We must take what we can and flee! Hurry, Joseph! Tell no one!"

I awakened the donkeys and packed only what

was absolutely necessary. Mary brought out the required baby things, and we piled them on the two beasts. There was no time to think. Within a single watch, we had wrapped our sleeping Jesus and begun our escape from Bethlehem. It would soon be dawn. Because of the visitors' gifts, we had the means to purchase what we would need along the way.

Before we left, I wrote a quick note to my apprentice, Gideon:

Dear Gideon,

May God be with you. Mary and I are forced to flee from Bethlehem. Our life is in danger, and I desperately need your help. I ask that you do the following. Take all our furniture and use it in your home. Find the money I have secreted under the one cubit plank near the fireplace. Pay my landlord his due and keep the rest for yourself. I hope to return someday, and if I do, to partner with you in our business. If I don't return within five years, the business is yours. Please delay talking about our departure as long as possible to give us ample time to escape.

In your debt,
Joseph

I decided to travel southwest. We reached the town of Etam before noon, and we stopped to rest. I was able to find room in the village inn. Since it was along the way, I inquired if there were any caravans leaving for Egypt. "Yes," the innkeeper responded, "See that man sitting by the fire? His name is Daniel. His caravan is completing its purchases and will leave soon. He will be following *Via Maris*, the route by the sea."

My request to join them was graciously accepted. There would, of course, be a small fee for the privilege. We would leave in two days and travel safely to Egypt. I shouted within myself, *God is great!*

The night before we left, word came that a massacre had taken place in Bethlehem. A priest had stopped overnight in David's city on his way home to Hebron. While there, he had seen a detachment of soldiers, sent from Jerusalem, enter the village. They systematically moved from house to house, searching for male children. He alleged, "Rumors were rampant. But I know for sure because I saw it with my own eyes. I saw soldiers taking a young boy from his mother's arms and slicing him with the sword." The priest quoted these words from the Holy Scripture:

A sound is heard in Ramah, the sound of bitter weeping. Rachel is crying for her children; she refuses to be comforted, for they are dead.

The priest continued to instruct, "These words of Jeremiah are a prophecy fulfilled in Rachel's town, Bethlehem, this very day. Something of enormous importance has happened. I don't know its meaning; but Jehovah will, in his own time, reveal it."

We learned later that only boys two years old and younger had been slaughtered. We also learned that it had something to do with King Herod's growing madness. Some said that he was seeking a child who could become a challenge to his throne; there was talk about this child being a universal king, a Messiah. My spine tingled! We were out of Etam by early dawn.

I had purchased a third and fourth donkey, one for Mary and one on which we fashioned a crib for Jesus. The bumpy, jogging gait of the donkey seemed to him a lullaby. He actually appeared to enjoy the trip. And, of course, Jesus became a favorite with the caravan crew.

Our journey was without incident. Since there were five other groups traveling with the caravan, when it was possible, we stopped in or near towns. On most stops we were able to find inns with available rooms.

After arriving in El Arish, many of the caravan guests began to go their separate ways. Since the main caravan was to pass through Tel Basta and on to Mostorod, we remained with it. This was the town we would call our temporary home. It had a large Jewish community.

After finding a house and settling in, my first task was to change the astronomer gifts into useful currency. I inquired among the faithful Jews for advice. Job, a highly respected elder of the synagogue, recommended me to a banker friend who worshiped at the temple. He proved to be an honest man. I was able to convert all three gifts into local currency. Most of it would be held safely in his bank.

Mary and I decided that since we expected to return to Israel, we should spend part of our time in Egypt exploring this land of our ancestors. We saw temples to various gods and statues of important pharaohs, especially Ramses II. And we sailed the Mother Nile. I suppose that the most awesome site was that of the pyramids and the sphinx. I still wonder how they were able to build them.

When our touring escapade ended, we returned

to the rented house and settled in for what we hoped would be a reasonably long stay; we expected to become part of the local Egyptian-Jewish community. Our home and hearts were full. Jesus was crawling all over the house and making sounds Mary and I liked to interpret as words.

Soon I was again practicing my trade.

But just as we were beginning to feel that Mostorod was our home, the inevitable took place—my night with God's angel.

It happened this way.

It must have been near morning. I awoke realizing that an angel had been in my presence. The recollection was very real. This time the angel had hovered over my bed as he spoke. His message was simple:

> *Get up, take the child and his mother, and go back to the land of Israel. Those who tried to kill the child are dead. Herod is dead.*

For some reason I remembered the words of the prophet Hosea when he wrote,

> *When Israel was a child I loved him and called him out of Egypt.*

We were gone within the month.

We again traveled with a caravan. My intent was to settle in Bethlehem again so I could partner with Gideon.

As I entered the carpenter shop, Gideon turned, smiled, and ran to give me the biggest hug ever.

"I'm so glad to see you. You have no idea how I worried. After Herod's soldiers slaughtered the little boys in our town and the neighboring farms, I knew why you had fled.

"I knew your Jesus was special, so special Herod needed him dead. But, I could never understand why that butcher chose to murder over twenty innocent babies just to make sure one special kid was dead. But that's all over. That fiendish butcher is finally gone."

Before I could speak, Gideon rushed on, "Joseph, I have honored your request. Your furniture is intact, a little more worn from use, but intact. Your carpenter tools are still in good shape, and I welcome you as my partner."

Finally I was allowed to say something. "Thank you. You are a good man, Gideon, and I am indebted to you. After finding accommodation in the inn and getting Mary and the child settled, you can help me find a house."

"For the time being," beamed Gideon, "why not

stay at my house? It's your old house. After you left and I paid your landlord, he offered that I should buy the property. Since it was next to the carpentry shop and since I had some money left from your hiding place, I agreed. And when you think about it, part of it is yours anyway, the furniture at least. There is plenty of room. You, Mary, and the child can share the large bedroom, and I will sleep next to the fire. I'm still a bachelor, and I yearn for the joy of family."

I agreed. We talked into the night. I learned that upon Herod's death, Caesar Augustus had decreed that he would not again appoint a single king of Israel. The realm would be divided, and each part apportioned to one of Herod's sons. Archelaus, with the title ethnarch, was awarded Judea, Samaria, and Idumea; Antipas, as tetrarch, given Galilee and Perea; and Herod Philip I, as tetrarch, assigned jurisdiction over the several minor states to the north and east.

As I inquired further, I learned that Archelaus was cruel like his father. King Herod had placed the Roman symbol, a golden eagle, above the entrance to the holy temple as his way of demonstrating Roman dominance over all that is Jewish, even the temple. Students of the righteous rabbis, Judas and Matthias, removed it. It cost them their lives. They were burned alive!

Soon another Judean cruelty brought death

to nearly three thousand Pharisees following a Passover riot. Then, while Archelaus was in Rome to be crowned, a group of messianic claimants incited numerous other rebellions. Military intervention followed, resulting in the crucifixion of at least two thousand people.

Judea was not a safe place to raise one who had been named Messiah. We could not stay. Once more the angel visited me with instructions. After discussing the problem with Mary, and sharing my dream, we agreed that returning to Nazareth was the best option. We still had some money left from the astronomers' gifts; it would provide for our needs until we could again settle—this time, hopefully long-term.

Our first stop was to the home of Mary's parents in Jerusalem. We were not able to warn them that we were coming.

I knocked on the door. After a moment, it opened. There was Joachim, aghast. He looked, he stared, he struggled to stand, and in obvious shock he stammered, "Anne, come here! Anne! A miracle!"

Anne came running; she saw Mary, leaped into her arms, and sobbed and sobbed. "Oh, Mary, we thought you were dead. We heard what Herod had done. We thought all of you were dead!"

Joachim gently pulled Anne away, "But you're alive! And Jesus is alive! Joseph, what happened to you? Where have you been? We've been half-crazy; we worried that you were dead!"

Before we could begin to explain, Grandmother Esmerentia, carrying a quilt in her arms, fairly sprinted toward the door. There was more hugging, kissing, and crying. Then Grandmother saw Jesus. "Jesus, my sweet dear child, give Great-Grandma a kiss."

As Grandmother whisked our baby into her arms, she exclaimed, "Well, little Jesus, guess what Great-Grandma has for you? Another bright, beautiful quilt, just like the one I gave you the last time you were here. And look. It even has donkeys and sheep and goats on it."

We asked about Grandfather. He had died peacefully in his sleep several months before.

After settling in, we talked. It was finally time to tell them—*everything*.

Mary began by describing her incredible visit from Gabriel, her miraculous pregnancy, her fortuitous visit to Zechariah and Elizabeth, the humiliation following her return to Nazareth, Joseph's compassionate understanding, the hidden reason for our trip to Bethlehem, the untimely birth of baby Jesus, and the amazing shepherds' visit.

I then explained what had happened after we left Jerusalem following completion of the redemption and purification rites. I shared the story of the astronomers and their gifts. I talked about my dream and how we had fled from Bethlehem for Egypt.

Mary then portrayed our life as part of a Jewish community in Egypt and our travels. Her description of the pyramids fascinated Anne.

After telling of the second dream, I concluded with the events following our return to Bethlehem and our decision to return to Nazareth.

Now Mary's parents and grandmother knew *everything*. They were overwhelmed!

Each event of the past two years was discussed, dissected, and reenacted. They gradually began to understand—Mary and I were to fulfill a plan from God. He had chosen us for something very special.

We stayed with Mary's parents and grandmother for several days and then began the trek to our hometown.

I thought, as we approached Nazareth, *Jesus will not have the status of one raised in Judea. He will be called a Nazarene.*

MATTHEW 2:13–23; JEREMIAH 31:15; HOSEA 11:1; LUKE 2:39

THEN MARY SAID

*I*t was truly a scary time. We feared for his life! What could have happened to Jesus? We were on our way home from Jerusalem, and Jesus was missing!

To help you understand what took place and why it happened, I need to tell you about our young boy, his *Bar Mitzvah*, and his first Passover.

Twelve is a very important age for a Jewish

boy. It is the time when he becomes an adopted son of the Law. Jesus' *Bar Mitzvah* is now past. It was a day of rejoicing. Three families joined us to observe and pray as four boys became young men, when they pledged to begin their walk with God as young adults.

Jewish practice teaches that each male child has three teachers: his mother until he is weaned; his father until puberty; the Torah through the rest of his life. Jesus had reached this third level. During the *Bar Mitzvah*, Joseph released himself as his teacher with the words, "Blessed is he who has now freed me from the responsibility of my son, Jesus." Our son would now be guided by the Torah. It would lead him toward the fulfillment of his predestined earthly mission.

I think that Jesus, since the time he could talk, knew he was different from other children. I often called him my "little king." Sometimes his father would take him aside for individual tutoring sessions. These times were special, for it was then that Jesus learned about the person known as Messiah, how he would be a great ruler, and how many people believed he would free us from the bondage of the Romans.

As his mother, I had many private moments with Jesus. He would sit next to me and listen intently as I told him stories about our people. The stories Jesus seemed to like best, those which fascinated him most, were the stories of Gabriel, our trek to Bethlehem, the shepherds, and the men from Persia. I can't tell you how often I retold them. I omitted the bad parts. Jesus was eleven years old before Joseph told him the story of the massacre in Bethlehem. He wanted Jesus to understand why we had had to move to Egypt.

By the time of his *Bar Mitzvah*, our son was already eagerly seeking his life's purpose. His free time was spent with the rabbi and Eli, our synagogue president. He would coax either of them who was free to help him search the wisdom of the Torah and of our fathers. He was full of questions: difficult, deep questions; questions about ideas, concepts, theories; notions far beyond the comprehension of normal children his age.

To his siblings he appeared obsessed; to many of his young friends, weird. Some neighbor kids even teased him with the name "Crazy Balaam." God was not showing him an easy path. He was in my prayers constantly. I wanted him to grow in wisdom and understanding. He had a brilliant mind. I hoped we, in our small town, were not stifling his mental growth.

The winter rains were ending, and it was time for

the Passover. Joseph and I went every year. This time Jesus also would attend. Our caravan left the day after Sabbath. We traveled slowly, stopping for rest and lunch, measuring our distance so we might set up camp shortly after the third watch. Following this pace we arrived outside Jerusalem the day before Passover Sabbath.

Our caravan set up camp on the Mount of Olives, just outside the northeast city wall. Men would spend the night under and around a tent in the area nearest the road, all women under a tent to the south, and the single young men clustered yet farther south. A lamb and other Passover necessities were purchased from the numerous vendor kiosks set up on all sides of the city. Soon it was sundown. As I looked about the mountain and the valley below, before me spread a sea of tents and campfires, with masses of people scattered about. These were God's children, the children of Israel, gathered to pay him homage.

Soon, the next day, all over the city and in surrounding areas, hundreds of Passover meal preparations were in progress. The Passover celebration would begin at the third watch and be completed before sundown. Our caravan group was able to gather around one table arrangement set up under the men's tent. Joseph built a campfire in an area between the men and women's tents shortly after sunrise. Now the Passover lamb could be killed and roasted over the fire. Women's energies were spent preparing foods such as eggs, bitter herbs, greens, *haroset*, and *matzha*. After all was ready, the meal began.

I can still remember the beginning of the introductory prayer: "Blessed are you Lord God, King of the universe."

With that, the ritual of the Passover began. Each of the foods was assigned a meaning, reviewing our slavery in Egypt, God's intervention, and our freedom. The events of the first Passover were our central focus. We remembered the ten plagues, each with a drop of spilt wine, especially the last in which the angel of death passed over all homes that were painted with the lamb's blood on the top lintel and side doorposts of the entrances. In these, the firstborn son was graciously spared. In all others he died. The meal ended with a fourth glass of wine followed by the pronouncement of Aaron's benediction to the children of Israel.

> *The Lord bless you and keep you.*
> *The Lord make his face to shine on you and be gracious unto you.*
> *The Lord lift his countenance upon you and give you peace.*
>
> *(Numbers 6:23–27)*

During the next days, our focus was on events inside the holy temple. Animals, grains, vegetables, and fruit were driven or carried to the Levites as offerings. Priests dashed about, overwhelmed with the pace they were forced to keep. Each day at the third and ninth hours, billows of smoke rose as sin offerings, guilt offerings, burnt offerings, trespass offerings, votive offerings, thank offerings, and peace offerings. All in honor to Almighty God!

Jerusalem is a grand and beautiful city. Its several towers and palaces stand out among the hundreds of stone houses and market structures. Most impressive is the holy temple. Built on a broad, flat mount high above the city, it reminds each pilgrim that this is the earthly *home of God*, the place where his Spirit dwells.

My grandparents had both died. Joseph and I could have chosen to stay at my parents' home, but one of my brothers was rooming there. And because my parents were quite old with health problems, it was decided the extra company would be a burden to them. We did, however, spend considerable time at their house. After a day visiting with them, Jesus asked if he might be freed to explore the holy temple.

He explained to us, "Now that I am a son of the Law, I need to become immersed in its wisdom.

From now on, I would like to spend all my time in the temple." We knew Jesus was intense in this desire, so after cautioning him to be careful, we gave our consent.

Joseph and I discovered Jesus missing the first night after making camp on our way back to Nazareth. The party we were traveling with was rather large. We inquired everywhere; no one had seen him. Joseph comforted me as best he could. We prayed; others joined us in prayer. I was comforted but worried. "What could have happened to him, Joseph?"

Early the next morning we started our return to Jerusalem. We began at my parents' home. No Jesus. We searched the area about the temple. No Jesus. We searched the temple. No Jesus. We returned to my parents' home for the night. The next morning we searched the temple again. There was Jesus, partially hidden among a group of scholarly men in intense discussion. What a relief. "Thank you, Lord!"

I ran to Jesus and cried, "Son, why have you done this to us? We've been looking all over for you. Your father and I have been terribly worried. This is our third day searching for you."

Jesus looked at me with a quizzical frown,

Mother, Father, why did you have to search for me? Didn't you know that I had to be in the holy temple, in my Father's house?

We had no answer.

Several days later, on our way back to Nazareth, Jesus told me the story of his Jerusalem adventure.

"My exploration of the holy temple led me through the Huldah Gate and into the Gentile Court. I hurried from place to place, bumping through the crowds as I explored every corner in the Court of Women. Since I was now a son of the Law, I was allowed to enter the Court of Israel. As I stood there with men from all over Israel, I could see the Court of the Priests, the holy place, and the holy of holies. It was so exciting! There I watched the priests and Levites as they prepared each animal or plant for sacrifice.

"After several hours observing what was happening, I began to look for some scribes and lawyers. I meandered here and there until I came to Solomon's Porch. This is where the scholars were meeting to discuss the Holy Writings. I wasn't sure it was proper, but I cautiously approached the area.

"No one stopped me. I sat near enough so I

could hear. They were discussing Job, debating the logic of Zophar's argument about God punishing those who are wicked. Mother, it was fascinating! This is what I had hoped would happen to me. The next day I found a group researching Melchizedek, king of Salem. He was a high priest, before Aaron, Mother. Some thought he would become the promised Messiah.

"Mother, you have no idea how wonderful it was to be among those learned men. I'm beginning to find some guidance toward discovering my life's mission. After the second day, I was so caught up in the debates I could think of nothing else. Then, guess what, Mother. These masters of theology began talking with *me*. They asked me questions. I answered. They treated me with respect as if I were as wise as they.

"The first nights I returned to camp, and in the morning, after chewing down a much-appreciated breakfast, I was immediately on my way to the holy temple. On the third day, when our discussion began to last into the night, two of these scholars asked if I would like to stay with them inside the temple. They had a room with cots. I agreed.

"There was so much to do, so much to learn; I totally lost track of time! I was doing what I had been born to do! This was my Father's business, Mother! I had to be in my heavenly Father's house!

"But, Mother, I promise to stay home with you and obey you and Father until I am a grown man. I am now old enough to help. If Father will let me, I will become his apprentice."

Only after a considerable reflective pause could I say to my husband, "Joseph, we are blessed and burdened with a son whom God ordained as Savior and Christ. I don't think we can successfully challenge anything he does. I have come to believe that our life's purpose is to open paths for our child; he must be what God has predestined him to be."

LUKE 2:40–52

But when the right time finally came, God sent his own Son. He came as the son of a human mother and lived under the Jewish Law, to redeem those who were under the Law, so that we might become God's sons.

(Galatians 4:4–5)

APPENDIX 1

Dr. Paul Maier writes in the first paragraph of his introduction to *Eusebius: The Church History, a New Translation with Commentary* the following:

Eusebius, Bishop of Caesarea (c. a.d. 260–339) is considered by many the father of church history. He was the first to undertake the task of tracing the rise of Christianity during its crucial first three centuries from Christ to Constantine.

In the section of Maier's translation entitled, "The Variant Genealogies of Christ," Eusebius shows how the genealogies of Matthew and Luke are both genealogies of Joseph (35–38). Eusebius postulates that Matthew identified the genealogy for physical descent while Luke identified the genealogy to express legal descent.

Eusebius quotes from two early church fathers,

Africanus and Aristides. In a letter written by Africanus to Aristides, Africanus states,

> *Matthan, Solomon's descendant, begot Jacob. When Matthan died, Melchi, Nathan's descendant, begot Heli with the same woman. Heli and Jacob thus had the same mother. When Heli died without children, Jacob raised up seed for him in fathering Joseph, his own natural son but Heli's legal son. Thus Joseph was the son of both. (38)*

The table generated by Dr. Maier illustrates the genealogical relationship (36).

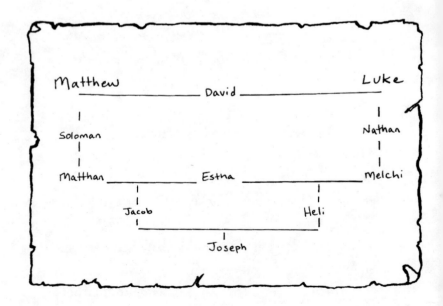

Maier, Paul L. *Eusebius: The Church History.* Grand Rapids, Michigan: Kregel Publications, 1999.

APPENDIX 2

NORTH

Great Sea

GALILEE

Sepphoris •

Nazareth •

• Caesarea

Beit Shean • *Jordan River*

SAMARIA

Sea of Galilee

PEREA

Jericho •

• Ein Karem

Jerusalem •

Bethlehem •

Etam •

Hebron •

Salt Sea

IDUMEA

◀ To El Arish & Mostorod

EGYPT

ISRAEL - NATIVITY LOCATIONS

DISCUSSION AIDS

You may wish to use *Narratives of the Nativity* for youth or adult Bible discussion. Below are questions that may be helpful.

Then Zechariah Said–Luke 1:5–23

1. To whom did the archangel Gabriel also appear? (Daniel 8:15–17; 9:20–22; Luke 1:26–27)
2. How might you, if you had been Gabriel, have responded to Zechariah's unbelief?
3. Name as many temple duties as you can that might have been assigned to priests. Which would you prefer as your assignment? (Lev. 1:1–9, 12, 14–15; 2:1–3; 4:32–34; 5:7–13)
4. Name as many temple duties as you can that might have been assigned to Levites who were not priests? Which would you

least prefer? (1 Chronicles 23:2–5, 27–32; 26:20)

5. If you had written "Then Zechariah Said," how would the content of the story differ?

Then Jacob Said-Matthew 1:1-17; Luke 3:23-38; Deuteronomy 25:5-10

1. How could Joseph be a son of both Jacob and Heli? (Appendix 1) (Deuteronomy 25:5–10)
2. How were engagements in Bible times and modern-day engagements similar? Different?
3. If you had written "Then Jacob Said," how would the content of the story differ?

Then Mary Said-Luke 1:26-39

1. Why do you think Mary was chosen to be the mother of God?
2. Why was it important that Gabriel informed Mary of Elizabeth's pregnancy?
3. Had you been Mary, how would you have dealt with this pregnancy?
4. If you had written "Then Mary Said," how would the content of the story differ?

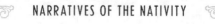

Then Elizabeth Said-Luke 1:24-25; Luke 1:39-56

1. Why was becoming pregnant so very important to a Hebrew woman?
2. How did sharing the two Gabriel stories become convincing evidence that both babies were very special gifts of God?
3. How would you support Zechariah's conclusion about the roles of each baby?
4. How does Mary's poem show she was very familiar with Old Testament Scripture? (1 Samuel 2:1–10)
5. If you had written "Then Elizabeth Said," how would the content of the story differ?

Then Zechariah Said-Luke 1:57-80

1. What obvious concerns did Mary have at this time?
2. What was the meaning of circumcision? (Genesis 17:1–14, 22–27; 21:1–4)
3. Who could be considered a Nazarite? (Numbers 6:1–21; Judges 13:2–7, 24; 16:15–17)
4. Was Jesus a Nazarite?

5. According to Zechariah's poem, what was to be John's earthly mission?

6. If you had written "Then Zechariah Said," how would the content of the story differ?

Then Joseph Said-Deuteronomy 25:5-10; Matthew 1:1-17; Luke 3:23-38; Matthew 1:18-25; Isaiah 7:14

1. Describe Joseph, the man.
2. Describe Mary, the woman.
3. Many Bible scholars believe that the two genealogies, Matthew 1:1–17 and Luke 3:23–38, are of Jesus through his legal father, Joseph. How can that be true? (Appendix 1)
4. If you had written "Then Joseph Said," how would the content of the story differ?

Then Caesar Said-Luke 2:1-3

1. In Paul's letter to the Galatians (Galatians 4:4–5), he writes, "But when the right time finally came, God sent his own Son. He came as the son of a human mother and lived under the Jewish Law, to redeem those

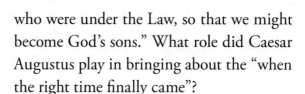

who were under the Law, so that we might become God's sons." What role did Caesar Augustus play in bringing about the "when the right time finally came"?

2. If you had written "Then Caesar Said," how would the content of the story differ?

Then Joseph Said—Luke 2:1-5

1. Through Joseph's choices, God's will was fulfilled. In what ways may you have been guided to make life choices that led to the fulfillment of God's will?
2. How large a town do you think Bethlehem was at this time?
3. How would you have coped with a stable as your temporary home?
4. How soon after arriving in Bethlehem do you think Jesus was born?
5. If you had written "Then Joseph Said," how would the content of the story differ?

Then Mary Said—Luke 2:6-20

1. Describe your reaction to Mary's delivery.
2. Describe what you think your reaction

would have been to the appearance of angels
if you had been with the shepherds.

3. Describe what you think your reaction
   would have been to the message of the
   angels if you had been with the shepherds.

4. Describe what you think your reaction
   would have been to the stable visit if you
   had been with the shepherds.

5. If you had written "Then Mary Said," how
   would the content of the story differ?

Then Joseph Said–Luke 2:21–38; Genesis 17:9–14; Exodus 13:1–2, 11–16; Numbers 18:15–16; Leviticus 12:1–8

1. Joseph was a carpenter. Why was it important that this be his vocation?

2. How does Jesus' circumcision relate to
   Galatians 4:4–5?

3. What was the purpose of the rite of redemption? (Exodus 13:1–2, 11–16; Numbers
   18:15–16)

4. What was the purpose of the rite of purification? (Leviticus 12:1–8)

5. If you had written "Then Joseph Said," how
   would the content of the story differ?

Then Gaspar Said–Matthew 2:1-2; Numbers 24:14-19

1. How did the heavens need to be configured before the wise men were sufficiently convinced that a special king had been born?
2. If you had written "Then Gaspar Said," how would the content of the story differ?

Then Herod Said–Matthew 2:1-10; Micah 5:2

1. Why was Herod called "Great"?
2. Why did the wise men come to Jerusalem rather than Bethlehem to find the King?
3. If you had written "Then Herod Said," how would the content of the story differ?

Then Mary Said–Matthew 2:9-11

1. What was the significance of a gift of gold?
2. What was the significance of a gift of frankincense?
3. What was the significance of a gift of myrrh?
4. If you had written "Then Mary Said," how would the content of the story differ?

Then Melchior Said–Matthew 2:12

1. If you had written "Then Melchior Said," how would the content of the story differ?

Then Joseph Said–Matthew 2:13-23; Hosea 11:1; Luke 2:39

1. Have you had a dream that changed a part of your life?
2. Why was it important that the holy family leave immediately?
3. Upon return from Egypt, why did Joseph choose to move his family to Nazareth rather than continue life in Bethlehem?
4. If you had written "Then Joseph Said," how would the content of the story differ?

Then Mary Said–Luke 2:40-52

1. How many dreams did Joseph have in which God's messenger spoke to him?
2. Imagine growing up as Jesus. What would be the high points and low points of your young life?

3. If you had been Mary or Joseph, would you have worried about Jesus' safety?

4. As a young man, Jesus knew he was special. When do you think he possessed a full realization of who he was, i.e., the Son of God, the Savior of mankind, the Son of the Trinity?

5. If you had written "Then Mary Said," how would the content of the story differ?